Confusion at time of NI's accession may be due to [...] took
place in camera vs. public involvement.

Rocky translation
awk!

CHSP
HUNGARIAN AUTHORS SERIES
NO. 1

EDITORS
Peter Pastor
Ivan Sanders

FALSE TSARS

Gyula Szvák

Translated from the Hungarian
by *Peter Daniel*

Foreword
by *Nicholas V. Riasanovsky*

Social Science Monographs, Boulder, Colorado

 Center for Hungarian Studies and Publications, Inc.
Wayne, New Jersey

Distributed by Columbia University Press, New York

2000

EAST EUROPEAN MONOGRAPHS
NO. DLV

Originally published as *Hamis cárok*
© 1988 by Szvák Gyula

© 2000 by Gyula Szvák
© 2000 by the Center for Hungarian Studies and
            Publications, Inc.
            47 Cecilia Drive, Wayne, New Jersey 07470–4649
            E-mail: pastorp@mail.montclair.edu

Copyeditor: Susan Kerestes

Library of Congress Card Number 00–130204
ISBN 0–88033–453–3

Printed in the United States of America

CONTENTS

FOREWORD   by *Nicholas V. Riasanovsky*   vii

Chapter 1   THE TERRIBLE "GOOD TSAR"   1

Chapter 2   A FRAUD ON THE THRONE   7

Chapter 3   FAKE FALSE TSARS   27

Chapter 4   IMPOSTORS ABROAD   47

Chapter 5   THE COSSACK LEADER AND THE
              INVISIBLE FALSE TSAREVICH   61

Chapter 6   THE ANTICHRIST TSAR AND HIS
              FALSE SONS   81

Chapter 7   EMPRESSES, MINIONS, IMPOSTORS   95

Chapter 8   A FOLK HERO IN THE ROBE OF A
              TSAR   109

Chapter 9   THE LEGEND DIES   131

Chapter 10   FROM TSAR GRISHKA TO OSTAP
              BENDER   147

NOTES   153
MAP   165
INDEX   167

FOREWORD

Professor Gyula Szvák's *False Tsars* is a very interesting book. It is essentially a summary treatment of almost countless pretenders to the Russian throne who claimed to be the rightful sovereigns of the country and the people, from the sixteenth century and especially the Time of Troubles to the twentieth. (It stops just short of the false Alekseis and Anastasias of our time.) The author emphasizes three major "waves" of pretenders: the numerous false Dmitris during and after the Time of Troubles (claiming to be Ivan the Terrible's son Dmitri who had died in childhood), the false Peters in the second half of the eighteenth century (following the death of Catherine the Great's husband Peter III in the palace coup of 1762) and the false Constantines of the nineteenth century (trying to assume the identity of Nicholas I's older brother Constantine who had been centrally involved in the confusing issue of succession following the death of Alexander I in 1825). In addition, Professor Szvák discusses or at least mentions very many other false contenders, who used a variety of names and operated at different times. Moreover, the author even pays some attention to claimants who aspired to less than the throne, and, indeed, to the entire issue of impersonation in Russian history in general. The short book is extremely rich, and even a close student of Russian history will find much to learn from it.

As to methodology, the author relies on primary sources, on the historical literature on his subject in several languages, and also on common sense. That last recourse may not entirely encompass his thoroughly fantastic material, but it is probably at least as useful as any other. Sometimes Professor Szvák gives more than one version of a particular episode. Always he tries to stay close to established facts. Thus he pays no attention to the opinion of the greatest historian of the Time of Troubles, Sergei Feodorovich Platonov, that the first False Dmitri was put forth by the boyars to destroy Boris Godunov, probably because that assertion, while it fits Platonov's brilliant social analysis, has no direct evidence to back it. Similarly, he neglects the view that the first False Dmitri believed himself to be the original Tsarevich Dmitri of Uglich. By contrast, we receive an abundance of attested facts. I was sad to discover that Marina Mniszech was not really a beauty.

In explicating and interpreting the phenomenon, or phenomena, of false tsars, Professor Szvák refers to a number of considerations and factors. Wisely he makes it clear that, broadly speaking, impostors operated in many countries throughout history, not only in Russia. Still, again wisely, he concentrates in considerable detail on the links between false claimants and tsardom. To be sure, the repeated readiness of the Russian people to rise in the name of the "true" tsar against the usurper on the throne resulted from the continuous poverty and oppression of the masses as well as the hope that the new and just ruler will improve their condition. Social uprisings became glaringly obvious in the Time of Troubles or in the great Pugachev rebellion of 1773–1774. Yet social protest in the name of the "true" tsar often seemed to follow a pattern of its own, and it needed a stimulus from above to become highly effective, such stimulus as the end of the dynasty leading into the Time of Troubles or the confusion over succession in 1825. While often utterly fantastic in their orientation and effort, the rebels in the name of the tsar still wanted to have a candidate of an appropriate age and with some physical markings indicating his tsarist identity. At the extreme, the presence of such a candidate, and occasionally even merely of his name, seemed to serve as a kind of formal seal to validate a rebellious movement, which in other ways defied all sense.

The events described in the book, both major and minor, throw much light on Russian economic, social, and even military history. Most intriguing, however, is the issue of tsardom itself and of its impact on the people. Without Kievan precedent, the emergence of tsar and tsardom marked the end of the appanage period and the appearance of Muscovy. The Mongols had no direct influence on it for they had very little in common with the Russians, never established their own dynasty in Russia, and were considered in Muscovy simply as divine punishment for Russian sins. Byzantium, of course, offered much more: Christianity came to Russia from Byzantium, and so did the title of *tsar* itself, originally Roman *caesar,* indeed in many ways Byzantium represented the religious, political, and cultural ideal for medieval Russians. But Muscovite tsars were not successors to Byzantine emperors. None of them ever made that claim; in fact, they rejected the offer of the Byzantine succession when it was urged upon them by others. As for the Russian masses, they had never been imbued with the Byzantine political theory. Some specialists wrote in general of the religious or quasi-religious nature of the Muscovite tsar and tsardom. But that approach can also create more problems than it solves. If one writes that the tsar was regarded in Muscovy as God or as the chief servant of God, one should realize that there is an immeasurable distance between the two identities. And the first is impossible in Christianity, in particular Orthodox Christianity. More appropriately one may conceivably refer to the emphasis in the Russian Church on the sacredness on this earth of everything associated with the divine. The tsar could share in that sacredness through the ritual of coronation, constant prayers for the tsar, the great deference accorded him in religious services and ceremonies, etc., etc.

Well, perhaps Professor Szvák will write his next book on the charismatic nature of tsar and tsardom in Russian history in general, not only as it applied to the fascinating deviant variant of "false" tsars.

Nicholas V. Riasanovsky
University of California Berkeley

Chapter 1

THE TERRIBLE "GOOD TSAR"

On miserable winter evenings the following tale is perhaps still being told to amuse Russian children:

When *Ivan* went his progress, many of the Commons as well as Gentry presented him with fine Presents: A good honest Bask-shoemaker, who made shoes of Bask for a *Copeak* a pair, consults with his wife what to present his Majesty; says she, a pair of fine *Lopkyes*, or shoes of Bask; that is no rarity (quoth he); but we have an huge great Turnip in the Garden, we'l give him that, and a pair of *Lopkyes* also. Thus they did; and the Emperour took the present so kindly, that he made all his Nobility buy *Lopkyes* of the fellow at five shillings a pair, and he wore one himself. This put the man in stock, whereby he began to drive a Trade, and in time grew so considerable, that he left a great estate behind him. His Family are now Gentlemen, and call'd *Lopotsky's*. There is a tree standing near his *quondam* house, upon which it is a custom to throw all their old *Lopkyes* as they pass by, in memory of this Gallant.

> A Gentleman seeing him so well paid
> for his Turnep, made account by the rule of
> proportion to get a greater Reward for a
> brave Horse; but the Emperour suspecting
> his design, gave him nothing but the great
> Turnep, for which he was both abash'd and
> laugh'd at.[1]

The story is simple and so is its moral: the good person is rewarded; the bad is punished. And in a folk tale, it is only natural that the good man is poor, hardworking and diligent; the bad is a lazy nobleman. There is nothing special to the tale, even in the fact that the tsar appears in the tale as the ultimate champion of right in all things, since both the structure and the moral of a great number of tales are similar—whether they focus on a king, an emperor, a caliph or a tsar. This is familiar almost everywhere in the world, appearing in the folklore of any nation at any time. It expresses the desire of the everyman before the industrial revolution to see the world around him change in a way that suits him. In many ways it resembles the religious anticipation of the Messiah, though, of course, it is much more down-to-earth. Herein is a popular utopia that expects happiness still in this world and can imagine justice only within well-known and reverently-respected bounds. The key role of the monarch is quite understandable: he is God's governor here on Earth and would certainly put an end to the despotism of evil landlords and officials—if only he know about it, if he did not live there in the capital, so far away from the simple folk. So let us open his eyes and teach a lesson to miserly lords and thereby restore his justice as well. By and large this is the very simplistic ideological pattern of popular rebellions in the Middle Ages. However naive, this unconditional belief in the "good" monarch may seem too omniscient in hindsight; however it was clearly the strongest popular ideology in pre-industrial societies. In this regard the Russian development is similar to that of other nations.

Naive monarchism, the belief in the "good tsar," emerged almost simultaneously with the institution of tsardom. The above little tale proves that Ivan IV, the first tsar of Russia* known as Ivan the Terrible, was also the first "good tsar." Thus the belief in the good tsar has a paradoxical nature even at its birth, initially being applied to one of the most loathsome figures in Russian history. Let us, however, not seek any controversy in this fact, as such legends are often born long after the death of the actual historical person—when his reign is already well shrouded in benevolent obscurity and he can personify the "good" and may be recreated through an embellishing popular memory, almost regardless of what actually happened during his reign. In fact, the above tale appeared not very long after the period it depicts, being collected in the imperial court in the 1660s by the English physician Samuel Collins (hence the world "shilling" in the story). Later we shall return to the question of what political interests were being served by idolizing Ivan IV in the early seventeenth century. Here we note only that certain groups at court must have consciously spread the tale in a wide circle to enhance the image of the terrible tsar. This was easy to do, as Ivan's homicidal campaigns against his immediate and less immediate entourage (that is, the *dvoriane*) were deeply imbedded in the collective memory. He was seen as the tsar who had even boyars killed, and this story could be set into the tripolar folklore pattern.[2] The Church also did its best to promote the image of Ivan IV, since the elevation of Russian grand princes to tsars produced a spectacular rise in the prestige of Church as well as that of the secular power. Even if the Russian tsar's influence on matters of religion cannot be compared with Byzantine caesaro-papism, almost all of them brought the church hierarchy under their jurisdiction. In Ivan's time, however, this state of affairs corresponded with the interests of the clergy, who could

---

*   "Grand Duke of all Russians" from 1533; "Tsar and Grand Duke of all Russians" between 1547 to 1584.

now claim that their country was more or less the only stronghold of the true faith—the Third Rome—and that they were conducting a kind of mission in trying to protect the Orthodox masses living far away from Muscovy. Through the consistent argument of the theologians, the doctrine of the divine origins and limitless authority of the tsar's power was thus shaped and hammered into all subjects with an astonishing speed, so much so that even one of the most tragic periods of Russian history, the "Time of Troubles," following the reign of Ivan the Terrible could not shake the faith in the authority of tsardom for a long time to come.[3]

Hardly sixty years after the coronation of the first tsar of Russia in 1547 and two decades after his death, the first direct attack on the sovereign's power was launched, inflicting deep wounds that took long to heal. The ideas concerning the good tsar had just emerged; the doctrine of God's anointed had barely taken roots, when the first attempt was made to undermine them. Was the recent concept of the good tsar still fragile? Hardly so, as the failure of the struggle to undermine it proves. Though a broad alliance of social classes topped the lawful tsar for a short time in 1605, justification for it was the elevation of a cunning tale to the level of doctrine and its evolution into a mass belief. This anti-tsar movement maintained that the sovereign was an usurper and that its own leader was the genuine successor. The real was fake, the fake was real. Thus, as a kind of reverse version of the belief in the good tsar, the ideology of Russian false tsars was born and was to live to the incredible age of two and a half centuries, producing countless—well, at least about a hundred self-appointed tsars—tsareviches and providing the belief that initiated all but one of the Russian popular rebellions.

Just as belief in the good tsar, a belief in the false tsar is not confined to Russian history either. False kings, pretenders, saviors are known to the history of almost every nation: examples can be drawn from ancient Egypt, from Rome, from medieval Europe. Some of these became relatively important figures in their own time, such as Perkin Warbeck who, enjoying foreign support in the last phase of the English dynastic struggle known as the Wars of Roses, caused considerable difficulties to King Henry VII. Unlike an earlier impostor, Lambert Simnel, who ended up as a scullion in the royal kitchens, Warbeck was taken seriously enough to be eventually executed.[4]

Others found a place in the hearts of the masses, such as the three false Jeanne d'Arcs who donned the maid's garb or at least rode her popularity years after her martyrdom. In particular Claude, the first of them, made quite a career by scrupulously harvesting a great deal of moral and, even more, material compensation for the sufferings of the heroine who died at the stake, presenting her bill wherever she could.[5] Another example can be taken from Hungarian history where false princes were also known. The legend of the "good Rákóczi"* was in full bloom during the eighteenth century, and several impostors claimed to be either Rákóczi himself or his son. It was no accident that, during 1735 peasant revolt of Pero Szegedinac, people took their oath to Prince Rákóczi. Although there is a strong similarity between the belief in the false Rákóczis and the false tsars, in Hungary it was much weaker. Unlike in Russia, the false pretenders and the popular movements never really connected with each other.[6]

In Russia, during a long period of its history, there appeared a huge number of false tsars and tsareviches. For this reason alone, their activities cannot be compared to the role of fake rulers elsewhere. Thus, when in the following pages we cover three hundred years of history of false tsars and tsareviches, attention will be paid to the uniqueness of Russian experience and mindset.**

---

* Prince of Transylvania and Hungary; he led one of Hungary's wars of independence (1703–1711) against the Habsburgs.

** I wrote this work in 1985 in Hungarian, which was published in 1988. Notes were added to this English language version. These include references to publications of the past ten years.

Chapter 2

A FRAUD ON THE THRONE

On an estate near the Russian border, owned by the Wisniowieckis, a powerful Lithuanian family, the household was fortunate to witness a "miracle" one autumn day in 1603. One of the servants, a ragged vagabond recently taken on by Prince Adam, was busy about his master's bath but, obviously not diligent enough, received a ringing blow from the prince. This was nothing out of the ordinary; but everybody was stunned when the servant burst out, "Should you, Prince Adam, know who I am, you would certainly not call me a son of a cur and even less would you slap me for such trifles! But I must bear my burden now that I have become your servant!" The surprised prince must have asked, "Why, who are you?" instinctively and, instantly, the bait was taken.[1]

The prince had no way of knowing that his man had already knocked at the door of many a nobleman's house to reveal his "secret." His first stop had been the Petchersky monastery in Kiev where he pretended to be mortally ill and breathed his precious information as his "last words"; he then tried his story out on the voivode with the same result as at the monastery: he was immediately thrown out. His next stop was in the house of a gentleman named Hoisky at the community of Goshcha where he seems to have made no revelation, as there is no record of his being ejected — though some sources seem to say that he was a diligent scullion there.[2]

What was the closely-held secret that tried so hard to pass our hero's lips but whose revelation had so far produced such drastic consequences? No doubt this story made bigger news than the birth of a one-eyed calf in the neighboring county or the appearance of a comet as recorded in chronicles. The servant stated nothing less than he was not a servant but a tsarevich, and no simple tsarevich at that, for his father was not an ordinary tsar but the terrible one who had died twenty years earlier.

The erstwhile scullion certainly profited from his earlier failures to the extent that he was able to fabricate a pretty story of his trials and tribulations. This was not easy, as it was common knowledge that not one of Tsar Ivan's three sons was still alive. Ivan killed his eldest son in a sudden rage in 1581. The second son, a halfwit, had survived to become tsar and died relatively young from (insofar as can be traced) natural causes in 1598. Dmitri, the youngest son, had died even earlier, in 1591. The circumstances of his death, however, were so hazy that some manipulation of the facts was possible. The question, of course, was not whether the boy had really died or not: that was clear to everyone. But as to how he died, there were several versions in circulation. According to the official investigative commission, the child had been seized by a bout of his recurring epilepsy and inflicted a fatal wound on himself during a knife-throwing game in the palace courtyard. Contemporary sources, including the minutes of the investigation, feature this version. Nevertheless, in the course of time a number of historians expressed their doubts, mentioning mostly the argument that the testimony of witnesses had been prefabricated. The reexamination stated that Dmitri's demise was in the interests of Boris Godunov, brother-in-law of Fedor, the halfwit tsar. It may be suspected that Godunov had the young tsarevich killed. Since the dynasty came to an end with Fedor seven years later in 1598, the road was open to Boris to assume formally the supreme power.[3]

We cannot tell what really took place that spring afternoon in 1591 in the town of Uglich. It remains a mystery, a mystery that had the potential for being exploited. The only certain fact is that the tsarevich died. But is that what really happened? For after a score or so years, stands a youth in his twenties in the bathhouse of Prince Adam Wisniowiecki and insists that he is the supposedly dead tsarevich. No, he has not risen from the dead, he says, he miraculously escaped the hired killers sent after him by Boris Godunov. Somebody else was buried in his stead, and he was hidden, then spirited away. Forced to wander for long years, he had endured countless hardships before daring to tell the truth at last.

Cursed with a questioning rationality, the modern reader may ask whether Adam believed this tale. According to Konrad Bussow, a German who happened to be in Russia at the time, the crucifix hanging from "Dmitri's" neck allayed the prince's last doubts. That seems to have been a real tour de force: a bathhouse servant a moment ago, the young man now plunges into the pleasures of sharing a bath with his master, and they partake together the ceremonial dinner given in his honor.[4] We harbor the suspicion, however, that Adam Wisniowiecki was no more naive than the voivode of Kiev. It cannot be doubted that he felt he had found a gold mine. He obviously sensed that this story might cause much trouble to Russia or at least to its sovereign. And there was nothing Prince Adam desired as fervently as that. Because of their estates along the Russian border, the Wisniowieckis maintained a rather stormy relationship with the Russian state. The events of the following weeks show that he at least entertained doubts on the identity of this tsarevich. He acted as if a true prince of the blood had found his way to him and had no hesitation in informing his relatives and acquaintances, as well as (indirectly) Sigismund III, the ruler of the Kingdom of Poland and Lithuania. Yet when the king summoned the "Russian heir to the throne" in order to examine the case for himself, Adam delayed the journey in every possible way until in the end it never took place. This seems to support the hypothesis that the prince did not believe the fantastic tale and, in particular, had no trust in others believing it. Supporting the false tsarevich seemed too risky a venture to him, and finally sober consideration prevailed. He would be putting his honor in jeopardy if it turned out that he has supported an impostor.

Either Adam Wisniowiecki did not have a politician's eye or he was too wise to play with fire. Thank to Boris Godunov's successful policy of consolidation, Russia seemed to be overcoming the effects of Ivan IV's catastrophic policies, and the country of the tsars seemed, at least from the outside, to be strong vis á vis a neighboring rival. But the changing political winds blowing over the Kingdom of Poland and Lithuania affected even those that had less tolerance of realities. This fact escaped Prince Adam's attention but not that of a relative of his, Prince Constantin Wisniowiecki who undertook to escort "Dmitri" to Cracow.[5] His determination may have been reinforced by the fact that his branch of the family had by then turned Roman Catholic, and he had no scrupl :s in playing dirty against the God-made institution of Orthodox tsardom.

This "Dmitri" was astoundingly lucky after all. The throne of the dual Kingdom of Poland and Lithuania happened to be occupied just then by a sovereign who was not afraid to pursue adventurous policies and, despite the definite objections of the majority of his counselors, wished to provide the impostor with a role. At the very beginning of 1604 he ordered the chancellor of Lithuania to discover "the truth." The chancellor took his sovereign's hint and produced a man called Petrushka who was supposed to have seen the tsarevich in Uglich and now "recognized" Dmitri by the long wrinkle on one of his cheeks and by his arms that were different lengths.[6] Although he could not yet be officially recognized because of the senator's objections, Dmitri's road to the capital was now open.

The impostor was truly favored by fortune. On the way to Cracow, his mentor brought him to the castle of Sambor to visit his father-in-law, Jerzy Mniszech, the local voivode and senator. The two men found an ideal partner in each other. At that moment Mniszech happened to have fallen on lean times, as some of his estates had just been seized by the court for his failure over a number of years to pay the taxes of the district entrusted to him. The impostor realized that he had found his real patron, one who had considerable influence in the kingdom, who was also to produce a large private army through his numerous kinfolk and vassals and who was truly interested in supporting the venture. But what exactly was the venture to be? The false tsarevich's plans had probably crystallized and taken shape during the time he spent at Sambor. Even earlier he had made no secret of his objective of nothing less than "regaining his rightful inheritance," the throne of Moscow, from the usurper Godunov. For a long time his hopes had been centered upon small-scale guerrilla warfare in which Cossacks would have made up most of his army. He is known to have spent some months among the Zaporozhe Cossacks after his disappearance from Goshcha, persuading many of them to be his followers. It is also possible that it was there among the Cossacks that he concocted his story of his being a tsarevich, having heard their accounts of the wars fought on the side of an astonishing number of false Moldavian princes. At Sambor, however, the struggle acquired entirely new prospects, since the opportunity of war between the neighboring countries for "returning him to his rights" would be provided by Mniszech. So Dmitri continued to push his case and set forward some very convincing arguments to persuade the voivode. First of all he promised him money, a lot of money, and then certain privileges to be bestowed on him, should the venture to capture the throne of Muscovy be successful. In order to seal the bargain, he undertook to propose marriage to Mniszech's youngest daughter, Marina. This step reveals the false tsarevich's determination, as the would-be bride was far from being a beauty by the standards of the age. On the other hand, Marina too had to swallow hard. The long, scarlike line running along along her fiancé's cheek made her father's protégé resemble a pirate rather than the son of a tsar. Still, high politics coupled with Mniszech's financial situation gave their blessing to this "love match."[7]

Events now followed in a rapid sequence. On March 15, 1604, the king in Cracow received the "tsarevich" who, taking a passage out of Herodotus, compared himself to the son of King Croesus who had regained his voice after an extended period of muteness. Sigismund III did not seem to have been awed by his visitor's oration and did not formally recognize his claim, since doing so would have meant a clear violation of the recently signed twenty-year peace with Russia. Informally, however, he supported the pretender and averted his eyes when Mniszech began recruiting troops, even helping him financially by cancelling taxes due to the treasury from the Sambor district.[8]

The impostor made a similarly good impression on Papal Nuncio Claudio Rangoni who, after their first encounter, noted that he "...is exceptionally sharp-minded, a very fine speaker, has reserved manners, shows an inclination to study literature, is extremely modest and introverted."[9] It was in this vein that he informed the Pope Clement VIII who, for the moment, did not share his nuncio's enthusiasm. On learning of Dmitri, the pontiff recalled the various Portuguese pretenders each emerging as Sebastian. But on hearing that the Russian impostor had taken up the Roman Catholic faith and had promised to lead all his subjects into the fold of Catholicism, the pope's hesitations were stayed.[10] We can see again how clever our Dmitri was. A valet not long before, he now had a senator as a prospective father-in-law and a number of high-ranking supporters, not to mention the silent sympathy of both king and pope. He had managed to make his "royal ancestry" credible, no less. He successfully played his chosen role at a very high level, providing a veneer of feasibility for an otherwise rather flimsy story. And he had achieved this at a time when Boris Godunov's administration was stepping up its campaign to uncover his fabrication.

The government was, of course, late in its countermeasures. The false Dmitri had already exchanged letters with the pope and was in command of a fine little army when, in the middle of

August 1604, the Russians sent a certain Smirnov-Otrepiev to Cracow with the task of uncovering the impostor. Among other doings Smirnov-Otrepiev aired a document he brought within him which stated that the bearer was a simple *dvorianin* (serving nobleman) and the uncle of the person claiming to be a tsarevich. Thus, "Dmitri" was no relation to the real Dmitri or to the tsar's family.

Given the weight of his information, it is astonishing that this uncle arrived in an unofficial capacity and that he had been instructed to bring up the matter only in an incidental manner. We can see that even now Boris Godunov did not take the impostor seriously and felt it beneath his dignity to deal with him at a level of high politics. Consequently, "Dmitri" did not cause much of a stir in refusing to meet his "uncle," claiming that the tsar had obviously sent hired killers to get him.[11]

Smirnov-Otrepiev's venture thus ended in failure. On his return home the Moscow administration officially informed Cracow on its views concerning the false tsar: "Yushka Otrepiev, as he was called before being uncovered, this degraded son paid not heed to his father's word, became a heathen, a thief, a robber, gambler and drunkard, often fled from home and finally, being unmasked, joined a monastery."[12]

Simultaneously, a meticulous investigation started into the background of the pseudo-tsarevich. The appointed officials took years to complete the task. According to their findings the impostor calling himself the Tsarevich Dmitri was a fugitive monk named Gregory Otrepiev. Arriving from Lithuania, his ancestors had settled in Galich and Uglich and were later granted an estate in Kolomna. Gregory's father died early, and his mother sent him to Moscow where he soon excelled himself in calligraphy. However, he did not choose a priest's life; instead he offered his services to the Romanov family, already influential at the time. When they fell out of favor in 1600 with Boris Godunov, the servant found haven in a monastery near Moscow. He was now resolved to become a monk. Soon he made a spectacular rise, transferring at first to Moscow's famous Chudov monastery, then even higher to the court of the patriarch where he was a confidential servant of the patriarch, frequently entrusted with errands even to the Boyar Duma. We have no incontrovertible information on his reasons for fleeing from here across the border. In the official version he did so because he had become a "heretic"—but that is too vague an explanation. He may have not wished to end his days in a monk's habit; he may have been driven towards adventure by an insatiable ambition.[13]

Years later Varlaam, another monk, told the tale of Grishka's escape. Walking along Moscow's Varvarka Street in the second week of Lent, 1602, he met his fugitive colleague. Without preliminaries Grishka suggested setting out together for the Holy Land. Though this was not an easy venture from the Russia of those days, they set off with a third monk they encountered on their way. At first they begged on behalf of a non-existent monastery, trying to collect money for the pilgrimage, then crossed the border. For a short time they stayed together; then "Grishka" deserted them, and the journey to the Holy Land was abandoned. The creditability of this account is much enhanced by an entry featuring the exact date and the names of the three monks in a book of the Zagorovsky monastery in Volhynia. Even Dmitri's account names several stages of his wanderings in Lithuania that match Varlaam's report. For this reason most historians accept the contemporary official identification of the false pretender. To consider all sides, however, we must remember that this identity was not proven by any legal examination and is therefore a post facto supposition.[14]

The investigating commission sent to Uglich in 1591 only made one fact absolutely clear namely, that the true tsarevich was really dead. This "tsarevich" was thus indeed an impostor. Even so, he managed successfully. Exploiting the Polish king's sympathetic silence and his prospective father-in-law's energetic propaganda, he organized his forces and in the autumn of 1604 was already on Russian territory. Was it megalomania that drove him towards Moscow to recapture his "rightful inheritance?" After all, attacking an enormous empire with only thirty-five hundred men can only be explained as being suicidal. With this in mind, Tsarevich Dmitri's delusions of grandeur are hardly in dispute. The former scullion had secured for himself permanent haven in the Kingdom of Poland and Lithuania as the exiled pretender to the throne of the neighboring rival power. Rather than staying put, however, he took his chances and went on the offensive.

We do not know his exact motives, but in his own special way he must have been a determined man. His fabrication seems to have taken on a life of its own; the role had overwhelmed the man. He had no self-control to resist the temptation of opportunity but had enough strength to withstand the bloody confrontations.

Inspite of having incendiary pamphlets smuggled across the border to prepare his arrival, even the "tsarevich" could not have thought he would reach Moscow in a triumphant march. Perhaps he was dimly aware that, at most, Russians living near the border would react favorably to the news of his appearance; but we should not assume that he realized that Russia was weakened by social tensions that were about to explode.

These social problems had their roots in the reign of the much maligned Ivan the Terrible. Besides exhausting the realm's human and financial resources in a twenty-five-year-old war for Livonia, the despot compounded the destruction by homicidal campaigns against his perceived domestic enemies. His violence was fueled by his paranoia. The population reacted to the catastrophe in the only way they could—by scattering in flight. This was comparatively easy on the endless Russian plains. The destination was often the Cossack settlements along the major rivers. Consequently, economically vital areas turned into wastelands; the landowners residing there lost the peasants who tilled their lands and became incapable of waging war. All that inevitably led to the weakening of the Russian state and army and, finally, to a decisive military defeat.[15]

Boris Godunov must have been aware that a policy of terror should be followed by a policy of consolidation. The speedy way of strengthening the state was to create a crack army that is, to settle the dvorianstvo's social and economic role. This could only be done in one way, by eliminating the still existing right of peasants to move, binding the workforce to the soil. Realizing what had to be done, in his capacity as Tsar Fedor's "brother-in-law and fellow sponsor," Godunov suspended the peasants' right of free movement for a year on several occasions. For the time being, this ban on the movement of peasants was still temporary; yet, the Russian system of perpetual serfdom was established then and there. Nevertheless, there were huge gaps in this institution. A perfect bondage was impossible as long as peasants had the opportunity to escape from under the authority of the decrees. They had three practical ways of doing so: running away to the free Cossack settlements, becoming border guards along the Russo-Lithuanian frontier, or ridding themselves of their peasant status simply by selling themselves to noblemen of high rank as household slaves.

The consistency of Boris Godunov's policy is demonstrated by the measures he took to close loopholes. He attempted to employ some of the Cossacks in registered government service and declared the rest outlaws. He forced the peasant soldiers living along the southwestern border to perform labor service (*barshchina*) on the endless "state-owned" plains there. Finally, in a decree dated 1597 he removed the benefits of serving a lord by decreeing that anyone spending at least six months as a slave would remain one to the end of his life. The same applied to debtor slaves regardless of whether they had paid their debts or not.[16]

That was an undeniably rational series of measures, even if the Russian people had to pay a very high price for it. It was also the first time in Russian history that society was divided into two opposing camps. Using traditional terms, we could say that the two basic groups of feudal society, those of the privileged and the subordinate, turned fatally upon each other. The tsar had nothing to worry about as he was able, with his well established organs of oppression, to smooth away social tensions, even though fortune did not always smile on him. In the year 1601 Russian was hit by a disastrous famine which claimed hundreds of thousands of lives and raged for another two years. This shift in the balance between good and bad years for agriculture occurred everywhere in Europe but struck especially hard in Russia which, it turned out, had not yet recovered from the economic crisis of the second half of Ivan IV's reign. People died in droves, and masters dismissed flocks of servants whom they could not feed. Roads filled with highwaymen and with the corpses of those who had starved to death. The first rebellion fueled by famine broke out: a slave, Khlopko organized his homeless fellow-slaves into an armed band in the south. They even reached Moscow but there they were easily scattered by the tsar's regular troops. So even in emergencies the tsar's organized methods of restraint were adequate to the task. The army of slaves, lacking a real leader, ideology, clear purpose or organization, were no match for the tsar's armed forces.[17]

This is why at first, only a year after the events above, when another hostile armed body appeared against him, it was only natural for the tsar to think that he would rid himself of it easily. He was so sure of himself that he boasted he would break the false pretender and all his retainers with a single finger. But the situation now was hugely different from the previous one. As soon as Tsarevich Dmitri crossed the border, hordes of peasants, Cossacks and slaves began to flock to him.

Had a radical change occurred since Khlopko's rebellion of the year before? Hardly so. The problems tormenting society were still the same, but deep-running opposition was now surfacing in drastic forms. The spontaneous resistance of peasants and slaves was being organized into a movement through a uniform belief. Ideology and leader became one. The impostor challenging the throne had no idea what a fertile soil his lies would fall onto. Not even in his wildest dreams could he have thought that by his mere appearance he could trigger popular resistance. With hindsight, of course, it is easy to declare the train of events being inevitable. There was the mob whose belief in a good tsar was like a religion and who thus would not take up arms against him though it had good reasons to do so. People believed the spreading rumor that the tsar on the throne was an usurper and that their leader was the rightful heir—the "good tsar." There was now no longer anything to prevent them from attacking the tsar. The "doctrine" of the false tsar had come into being and, without shaking the Orthodox subjects' belief in the "good tsar," functioned as an ideological framework within which larger groups could form in the struggle against supreme authority.

Did the crowd swallow so many uncanny lies simply because they wanted to believe them? Not at all. The lie had to be credible. To act on it, one needed a deep identification with it and had to have a true sense of calling. In this sense Grishka Otrepiev was clearly talented. In the Kingdom of Poland and Lithuania he had showed his ability to carry on, but his true opportunity to live out a lie came here, in Russia.

In the beginning everything went smoothly. The main army crossed the border at its farthest point without hindrance. The troops in the smaller forts swore allegiance to the "real" tsar without offering resistance. The Cossacks who joined Dmitri were on the march along the so-called Crimean Road, east of the main host, and drew the population and the soldiers of the mostly newly-built fortifications to Dmitri's side. Dmitri did not even have to take an active role. His name and story were enough. At Novgorod-Seversky, however, they met some resistance, and Godunov's administration was slowly awakening to the peril; a large army was sent out against the rebels. However slow the tsar's regular army was in coming, and however sluggishly it fought under its hapless commanders, the eventual battle delivered the inevitable defeat to the pretender. His Polish mercenaries, who had constantly been nagging him for money, left him and the rest of his army took a disastrous beating at Dobrinitch on January 21, 1605.[18]

Grishka Otrepiev, alias Dmitri, managed to escape with only a few of his followers to the fort of Putivl where, with nothing better to do, he waited for his luck to change. Fortune did come again to his rescue, for the government troops stopped neutralizing the remaining pockets of resistance. Some of them scattered in the countryside; others began to "discipline" the inhabitants of the territories that had taken the tsarevich's side. The main force was occupied in besieging Kromi, an insignificant fortress, with no great success.

In the meantime, despite the defeat of the main army the Cossacks in the rear of Kromi continued taking fortresses on behalf of Dmitri. The "tsarevich" plunged into feverish work. His incendiary manifestoes turned up even in the remotest corners of the country; his propaganda slowly captured the whole army set against him, from boyars to foot soldiers. Most essentially, his troops took great pains to maintain good relations with the population, while the tsar's soldiers engaged in their usual casual looting of the homes of peaceful peasants. Dmitri's men appeared as genuine liberators in the eyes of the victims. The false tsarevich was doing what was expected of a good tsar, and the people thus had no hesitation in seeing him as their real tsar. Dmitri's frequently staged spectacular bouts of piety also helped; he was careful to ensure that his fervent prayers always enjoyed the largest audience possible, which of course knew nothing about the Jesuit fathers swarming around the Orthodox tsarevich, even in his camp.[19]

Hating Boris Godunov for his lowly origins, the boyars started a whispering campaign against him. The army was becoming demoralized, and the people of Moscow were triggered by Dmitri's declarations into an excitement that threatened revolt. The ground was slipping out from under the feet of Boris Godunov. He introduced martial law in the capital and now he did in fact hire assassins to deal with the tsarevich. The torture chambers operated round the clock. From the sources, it seems clear that the events of these last months destroyed Godunov's nerves; falling into apathy, he hardly ever left his palace and used terror to counter his uncertainty and fear. It is no surprise to historians that the tsar, constantly ill since 1602 and having survived a stroke in 1604, died unexpectedly on April 13, 1605.[20]

All circumstances played into the pretender's hands; all the factors on which events turned had come out to the false tsar's benefit. The tsar's death was all that was needed for the Godunov system, shaken to its foundations, to collapse overnight as if by magic. After the long months of waiting, things began to happen to Dmitri in a breathtaking sequence. The army still besieging Kromi swore allegiance to him. The people of Moscow, aided by the boyars, broke into the Kremlin and killed Fedor, Godunov's son and heir. The boyars sent delegates to "Tsarevich Dmitri" to assure him of their loyalty. Having assumed the role of a popular leader, Dmitri suddenly found himself heading a broad alliance; the entire society took his side, as was a tsar's due. The remainder of his journey was a triumphal march to Moscow and to the throne of Russia, which he came to occupy with pomp and circumstance on July 21, 1605.

What had caused this turn of events? However credible his story of royal ancestry may have sounded to subjects living far away from the tsar's palaces, and however much the bottom layers of society were impelled to have faith in the impostor who promised them salvation, these were certainly not considerations that swayed the boyars' decision. During his stay at Putivl, "Dmitri" was generous with promises to all and sundry, offering freedom from taxes to the peasantry, freedom from bondage to the slaves and serfs, and money to the Cossacks. Now he gave rich grants to the nobles who had taken his side and declared the boyars' traditional rights inviolable. The latter were hardly satisfied though. Yet, their behavior is easy to explain; sensing popular unrest, they regarded loyalty to the impostor as a safe tactic, all the more so as he, after all, was pushing their cause. The bottom layers of society had done all the difficult work for them, toppling the hated Godunov regime without the boyars having to lift a finger. Now the boyars had at last the long-awaited chance to redistribute power. None of them doubted for a moment that Dmitri was an impostor and that they could easily convince the public of this when they wanted to.

This type of reasoning is backed by the fact that three days after the triumphant march into Moscow, Vasily Shuisky, who had headed the Uglich investigation commission, had to be arrested for disseminating the rumor that "Dmitri" was a self-appointed tsar. The time was obviously too early for cards to be laid on the table. The entire society viewed Dmitri as its redeemer and was looking forward to seeing his generous promises kept.

Before acting on the policy, the tsarevich had, as a matter of course, to dismiss the last doubts concerning his origins. He was now facing the most delicate test of all: having his tale confirmed by the one and only person competent to do so, the mother of the real tsarevich. The exiled Maria Nagaia had once been summoned to appear before Boris Godunov himself when in her troubled mind she had started doubting what really had happened at Uglich in 1591. Thirsting for vengeance, Maria then had not excluded the possibility of her son's being alive. Now the impostor took a seemingly terrible risk, as Nagaia could easily have exposed him before the entire world. But the pretender first met her in secret and staged the moving grand scene in public only when he was assured of her positive response. The former tsarina was quite willing to recognize him as her son, which obviously meant an end to her detention and the resumption of her high status. In her turn she confirmed "her son's" version of the facts, legalizing the sovereign rights of the false tsar. The coronation could now take place. As with all "good tsars" in general, the new ruler became divine immediately. We are witnessing a folk tale come true: a low-born but clever and ambitious youth endures hardships at the end of which, out of "the grace of God," he becomes the reigning tsar.[21]

In his fantastic rise, however, there were also the seeds of his easy fall. One cause of Grishka's tragic end was, paradoxically, his becoming tsar not only through acquiring unlimited power but also through self-fashioning, he became a monarch in his own heart. His fantastic goal dominated his whole being and when, in the unluckiest moment in history, the impossible dream was fulfilled, he himself could not escape the spell of the tale. He felt a genuine avocation to rule and was convinced he was qualified for the office. Indeed, he had good reason to believe so. In terms of ability, he was no worse than the tsars before and after him, and as a matter of fact, he surpassed many of them. If our judgment of him is flattering, it can be explained by his being on the throne too short a time for his acts as a monarch to be assessed. All we have is his intentions, and these can be documented with no little difficulty.

It seems certain that Tsar Dmitri had fully assimilated the doctrine of the unlimited power of Russian tsars and exercised his rights accordingly. He became as drunk with the power that fell in his lap as he had previously been patient and tactful as a pretender. The impostor's megalomaniac impudence can be seen in the statement he made that most of the crowned rulers of Europe were inferior to him but that he would gladly measure his strength against that of Alexander the Great. Of course, his Russian subjects were fully used to their sovereigns exercising the power of the tsar to maniacal extremes but we cannot tell how they would have reacted to some of his reforming ideas which, however, remained on the drawing board to the end. He definitely wished to broaden the rights of the nobility along Polish lines. He intended to establish a kind of senate and to found schools (perhaps a university). One foreign witness even noted that in the Boyar Duma the tsar resembled a schoolmaster among his pupils.

Dmitri's pipe dreams would hardly have disturbed the Russian public, unlike some of the measures he did take. It all started by his becoming too much of a tsar for the highest ranking nobles, since at the very beginning of his reign he endeavored, as all tsars should, to win the favor of the serving nobles. According to his Polish secretary Jan Bucinski, in the first six months of his reign, Dmitri distributed seven and a half million rubles among them, and even more importantly, he published an edict ordering that all servants who had escaped within the last five years and five months were to be hunted down and returned to their masters. The edict did, in fact, win over most of the dvorianstvo, but it turned against him those southern landowners, formerly his staunch supporters, who were harboring the fugitive kholops who had fled there at the time of the "great hunger." Naturally, the slaves themselves were least satisfied with the edict. Nor were they made happy by the decree of January 7, 1606, which liberated many of them though leaving even more of them in servitude. The landowners were outraged to learn that the tsar's administration was preparing new legislation that would restore the peasants' rights of free movement.[22]

We therefore cannot find a clear, straight line or the expression of a clear class interest in Dmitri's domestic policies. The essence was that he intended to keep all his promises and gave a little to everyone, which, of course, did not satisfy anybody. Thus the False Dmitri's "politics above classes" induced society, which had supported him almost to a man, to turn against him unanimously.

On the surface, of course, it was the tsar's private life that received the heaviest criticism. Dmitri was fond of his drink and women, which was all right as it went, but he even danced during his orgies. And after lunch, instead of napping, he took part in war games and bear fights. What is more, he was even fond of lamb! These were outrageous habits in Orthodox eyes, strengthening the terrible suspicion that the new tsar was breaking with tradition and making unpardonable concessions to foreigners (Catholics). The final straw was the arrival of Marina Mniszech, his bride, who at long last turned up in Moscow to be led to the altar by "Dmitri."

The wedding ceremony seemed to confirm the weight of religious doubts, since the tsar had an extremely complicated ceremony organized that bewildered all who attended. Everybody became aware of the shocking, unprecedented fact that the young Polish noblewoman, crowned as "Tsarina and Grand Duchess of all Russians," had become the Russian tsar's wife without converting to the Orthodox faith. To top it off, her three thousand strong entourage behaved so outrageously in the Russian capital that their clashes with the local population became an everyday occurrence. Feelings were running high in Moscow. Realizing the opportunity at hand, on one morning of the noisy wedding feast, the boyars sounded the alarm in the town, shouting "The Poles are out to murder the monarch!" Then, amid the tumult as armed people hurried to the Kremlin, they killed the tsar. Dmitri by the way, did not go easily—he jumped out of a window of the palace. Attempting to land on a wooden stand in the courtyard, he fell beside it crashing onto the flagstones. For a moment his luck, once again, seemed to have held, as he did not die of his injuries and a cohort of guards made a defensive circle around him. This time, however, the boyars did not wish to add yet another miracle to Dmitri's already impressive record. They threatened the soldiers with the slaughter of their families if they failed to hand over the impostor. They then shot the wounded man out of hand.[23]

This was the unholy end that befell the first and most successful of the false tsars in Russian history. As such he deserves our recognition, since even though aided considerably by his circumstances, he invented, shaped and realized a fantastic tale. Along with the tales of princes conquering fire-breathing dragons, it might be just another bedtime story, were it not true to the last detail.

Grishka Otrepiev the defrocked monk really did become a tsar and took his role seriously. He thus has to be judged also as one of the Russian tsars. There is no doubt about his personal abilities, shown in part by demeanor. He had a relatively wide understanding of the world at large and was aware of foreign countries, which makes him stand out from the tsars preceding him. Nor can we charge him with what he is often charged with—being in the pocket of the Poles and the Holy See. True, as a pretender he promised them everything, as he did to all; but once in possession of the powers of the tsar he reneged on these promises. As with the Russian tsars of all eras, his foreign policy consisted of defending the country's territorial and social integrity. Making his imperium vulnerable to foreign powers would have tarnished his belief in his own greatness,

What he can be blamed for is remaining all his life what he really was, an adventurer. Not that he had gambled away the country entrusted to him; but drunk with power, he abandoned the tactful and cautious behavior he had previously displayed. Similarly his attractive initiatives and strategic plans were stillborn. Even as tsar he had only one political credo: to use and abuse the power that unfathomable fate had dropped into his lap, to exploit all the pleasures offered by the post, to drink its dazzling nectar to the last drop without a second thought. His reign suited his nature: he gambled everything he had for eleven months on the throne. First he won, then he lost.

Chapter 3
FAKE FALSE TSARS

With the impostor out of the way, the boyars thought they were over the hardest part of their plot. Two days later they chose Vasily Shuisky, one of their number, as tsar. The false tsar's corpse wes dressed up in a clown's costume and laid out on Red Square for everyone to see. As far as the boyars were concerned, the affair was over: they had proved the falseness of Dmitri, had done away with him and now everything could go on as it had in the good old days, they thought. They were to be sadly disappointed in these expectations.[1]

It all began with a large number of purported miracles at the grave of the false tsar, who had been buried outside the city walls. Quickly, the authorities had the body disinterred and burned, the ashes mixed with gunpowder and shot out of a cannon aimed in the direction from which Dmitri had arrived to Russia. But his fame could not be extinguished by cannon fire. The capital was soon flooded with pamphlets reporting on the tsar's miraculous new escape. People were beginning to doubt that it was really Dmitri that they had seen dead on the city's main square. The tsar's Polish servant swore that a small fat man had been shot dead, not his master. It was also rumored that three horses had disappeared from the tsar's stables on that fateful morning. Naturally there were immediately people to claim that they had seen somebody closely resembling the sovereign galloping away. Such and similar rumors spread like wildfire, soon coalescing together and laying the foundations for the mood of the populace that was receptive to the next "miracle."

As usual, the "miracle" had a most rational explanation. The shadowy morning rider was Mikhail Molchanov, the false tsar's ill-famed confidant, who hardly stopped to rest before he crossed the Polish border. On the way he took great care to keep himself shrouded in mystery. Letters bearing the tsar's seal were arriving from Prince Shakhovskoi, who was exiled as governor to the fortress of Putivl by the new regime: he had simply stolen the seal. That, of course, was merely a trick. Shakhovskoi was the hand that reached out to save the legend from perishing along with the person who embodied it.[2] The medium in which the new tale was kept alive, however, was still that of a society seething with anger. The legend's vitality was ensured by the failure to remedy during the few months that had passed the grievances of the various layers of a society that were in revolt against the tsar. The false Dmitri was killed too soon. He had not been tsar long enough to personally undermine his own image and credibility in the eyes of the masses. For this reason his name became instrumental in launching another wave of resistance. The Shuisky administration made the mistake of exiling the false tsar's most faithful aides to the south, the area which had provided Dmitri's popular base. This resulted in the southern periphery's becoming practically independent of the government in Moscow from Shuisky's time onwards.

The leading group of boyars now had some idea of the real effect and importance of the false tsar's tale. A heavily ideological counter-propaganda was launched. As regards the assiduity of his communications, Vasily Shuisky was not an inch behind Shakhovskoi; he circulated his denunciatory writings in the names of the boyars, Maria Nagaia, and himself, even having a polemical piece fabricated about the false Dmitri's real life and deeds. Being not only a man of words but also of spectacles, he staged a peculiar show that bears witness to his originality. "Don't you believe Grishka Otrepiev was a common impostor? Well, I'll show you then!" must have been his idea, and he had the corpse of the real Tsarevich Dmitri, killed fifteen years before, brought to the capital from Uglich. But the miracles occurring at the coffin that arrived in Moscow were just as impressive as those that had taken place by the false tsar's grave. The little boy lying in the undamaged casket looked as if he had died only the day before. (Some people immediately seemed to know that an Orthodox priest's nine-year-old son had been sacrificed for this effect.) The dead child was still clutching the also fresh-looking nuts that he had played with on that fateful day. It is only natural that some of the "blind" regained their sight and some of the lame threw away their crutches in front of the casket. The show was followed quickly by the canonization of the tsarevich, then by the making up and spreading of a great number of miraculous stories about him. Tsar Vasily Shuisky could rest assured that he had done everything he could in the struggle against a phantom enemy.[3]

Actually, he should have done something about an enemy that stood with both feet on the ground. Moreover, he should have done even more about solving social problems. However, a keen mind was not in character of the elderly tsar. His opponents were riding the tide of the new opportunity. What makes the situation special was that nothing had changed since Grishka Otrepiev had crossed the Russian border and taken the Cossacks, slaves, serfs and peasants flocking into his camp. Actual social injustices and unresolved tensions were reflected in the situation. Belief in the false tsar was nourished by the general discontent and went farther than the previous anti-tsar movement had gone. The turn in the peculiar recurrence of events was provided this time by Ivan Bolotnikov, a fugitive slave.

We know very little about his background, and even less is known about the life of slaves. How and why he became one can only be guessed; but we know for a fact that he chose freedom over servitude and joined the Cossacks. During a raid, he was captured by Crimean Tartars and ended up on a Turkish ship as a galley slave. Luckily for him, this ship was boarded and pillaged in its turn by a German vessel. Landing in Venice, Bolotnikov started homewards. He had gotten as far as the Kingdom of Poland and Lithuania when an event changed his life.

On his way home he entered Sambor, where thanks to Molchanov and the wife of the Voevoda Mniszech, now a prisoner in Russia, many people believed in the legend of Dmitri's escape. It is only natural that Bolotnikov met Tsar Dmitri himself here. We are familiar with this famous encounter from the report of a contemporary German traveller, Konrad Bussow. Noticing that Bolotnikov was a seasoned soldier, the "tsar" suddenly "uncovered himself" and said to "his subject," "I cannot give you much now; here are thirty ducats, a sabre and a chestnut horse. Take this and take this letter, here, to Prince Shakhovskoi at Putivl. He will give you enough money from my treasury and make you commander of a few thousand warriors. You will lead them for me and, if God is merciful to you, set out against my foresworn subjects. Tell everyone that you have seen and spoken to me here in Poland and I am like what you see of me now, and that I myself gave you this letter to deliver."

Historians suspect that it was Mikhail Molchanov who assumed the role of Dmitri for the occasion and managed to hoodwink Bolotnikov, who had arrived from afar but had the support of several thousand Zaporozhe Cossacks. The former fugitive slave, in his turn, had no reason to doubt these words of Molchanov's, which legitimized his future military actions and elevated him to the rank of commander in chief (Bolschoi Woywoden).[4]

Thus, the Cossacks crossing the border now fought again in the name of Tsar Dmitri, and Bolotnikov's encounter with the "sovereign" gave a mighty impetus to the movement in the south, an area which had not yet accepted the new tsar and even fought his troops. Bolotnikov's arrival both strengthened the belief in Dmitri's escape and provided considerable military help, by means of which the rebels not only pushed the tsar's troops back but also went on the offensive and set off towards Moscow.

Two armies marched on the capital along different routes. The one led by Bolotnikov and gathered from the lowest layers of society could hardly be called an army. Their method of waging war was a curious mix of Cossack martial practice and medieval peasant revolt. They approached Moscow slowly and obviously laid an emphasis on teaching a lesson to the landlords they met on the way. Unlike them, the small army of service gentry led by Istoma Pashkov proceeded like a regular army, avoiding atrocities and referring any chance incident to the command center in Putivl. It was hardly an accident that, when they surrounded the capital in late October 1606, the two armies did not merge but made separate camps. A clash soon occurred between the two leaders over supreme command. Leading the larger army, Bolotnikov was the obvious winner and was able to have the "tsar's wishes" recognized relatively easily. Simultaneously, he revealed his rival of the task of negotiating with the envoy of Moscow's population. And now came the first time that belief in Dmitri backfired. The Muscovites seemed to accept all the harsh conditions but insisted on one point of their own. They wanted Tsar Dmitri himself to negotiate with them. Bolotnikov could only have a letter sent to Shakhovskoi, urging the prince to send the tsar at long last. He then settled down to wait.

This delay, however, favored Vasily Shuisky's faction, even though the success of the insurgent armies brought huge chunks of territory over to Dmitri. As if in response to the spectacular weakening of the Moscow center, fighting erupted in several areas of the country. What is more, the capital's residents closely followed and reacted to every turn in the struggle, which meant that the lawful tsar could not feel safe even in the Kremlin. But Bolotnikov's troops were unable to invest the town properly and even delayed storming it while an army was expected to arrive from Smolensk to relieve the capital. A great manipulator, Shuisky made the best possible use of his adversary's inaction. First he tried to buy off the commander in chief, and failing to do so, he persuaded Prokopi

Liapunov, commander of the Riazan serving nobles, to switch sides. With the number of deserters growing, the rebel army started to dissolve. Finally when Bolotnikov did risk a decisive battle, he was defeated. The main cause of his defeat was the betrayal of Istoma Pashkov, who also turned against him. The rebels were forced to retreat from under Moscow and take refuge in the fortress of Kaluga. With the movement abandoned by the last group of serving nobles, the further clashes could be considered as a clear conflict between social groups.[5]

Holed up in the wooden fortress, Bolotnikov repelled attack after attack by the tsar's forces but his strength was waning. All he could hope for was a miracle of some sort. Then, as if sent by Heaven, several thousand men appeared at Putivl, led by a Tsarevich Peter to relieve Kaluga. In his tight corner, Bolotnikov could not afford to question the identity of this tsarevich, who claimed to be the son of Tsar Fedor and thus the nephew of Dmitri, though perhaps even Bolotnikov knew that Fedor had never sired a son.

The instance of "Tsarevich Peter" displays an already prosaic feature of the spread of the false-tsar legend, followed by the emergence of new false tsars. It started back in the time of the false Dmitri, in the spring 1606. The Cossacks living along the river Terek started complaining loudly about the cessation of certain of their government subsidies. As always, the Cossacks, numbering three hundred, led by Ataman Fedor Bodirin, blamed the boyars: "The sovereign wanted to reward us but the cruel boyars do not give us our due." They were about to start on a minor looting foray near the Caspian but decided on another direction and to go towards Moscow along the river Volga in order to have their complaints settled. It is worth noting that they considered this venture possible only by having it "legitimized" by a false tsar. The Cossacks took a look round to see who could be assigned to that position. Their first choice was a fellow of theirs, a boy called Mitka, son of a *strelets* (musketeer) from Astrakhan.

Claiming, however, that he had never been to Moscow, Mitka turned his comrades down. The next candidate had no such scruples. He was Ileika (Gorchakhov) Muromets, bastard son of a hired hand from the Volga. So Ileika would be Tsarevich Peter, whose name drew all the Terek Cossacks to them. Peter was now in command of four thousand fighting men and felt strong enough to contact his "relative," Tsar Dmitri. The tsar's envoy gave his sovereign's answer to the Cossacks at Samara, inviting them to Moscow out of the obvious consideration of acquiring new support. However, on hearing the news of Dmitri's death, the Cossacks turned back, floating their horses down the Volga, and turned south-southwest to join their fellows on the river Don after a long and tedious journey. Here they received Prince Shakhovskoi's letter calling them to war. They did not hesitate: breaking camp, they rode to Putivl.[6]

The strength of the belief in the false tsar is demonstrated by the fact that the Shakhovskoi faction passed the command to Tsarevich Peter as soon as this "blood relative" arrived, despite their knowing whom they were dealing with. They were mutely obedient even when Ileika showed his real face and had a number of "unfaithful" service gentry butchered. But the governing princes' sacrifice was not in vain. While Bolotnikov at Kaluga continued to tie down Shuisky's main army, the rebels had a firm hold over the south and even had the power to launch a counteroffensive. Tsarevich Peter directed the struggle from his headquarters at Tula, and in March 1607 he finally managed to relieve Kaluga. To command the army that had rescued Bolotnikov, Peter chose Prince Andrei Teliatevsky, Bolotnikov's former master. It was a rare moment in history: a Russian lord and his slave fighting like equals for a common objective—but not side by side! As soon as they had driven off Shuisky's army, Teliatevsky brought his host back to Tula and thus made a renewed march on Moscow impossible. Bolotnikov had no alternative: along with his exhausted defenders he had to link up with "Tsarevich Peter." The rebels' passivity gave the tsar in Moscow yet another chance. With glittering gold coins and wild promises, Shuisky again had an enormous army recruited and took command himself. He made the pledge that Moscow's people would not see him alive again until he had dealt with the last rebel. His determination was understandable: influential groups in the city had long been considering the removal of the demonstrably incapable tsar; for him the campaign had thus become a matter of victory or death.[7]

Unlike Kaluga, Tula was a strong fortress with twenty thousand resolute men experienced in siege defense. Nevertheless, the rebels' hit-and-run maneuvers failed to prevent the enemy from investing Tula. An extended siege is usually advantageous to the besiegers, and indeed during the siege, the tsar's swarm of troops slowly but steadily neutralized resistance in the other territories under rebel control. The fate of the revolt under the banner of Tsar Dmitri was all but sealed when the tsar's camp was shocked to hear of news that came from the town of Starodub and revived the morale of Bolotnikov's men. According to reports, Tsar Dmitri had at last set off to aid his loyal, true-to-death subjects!

The truth was that the defenders' resolve was in taters after spending the whole of the summer of 1607 fighting. They grumbled endlessly and wanted to see the sovereign they were fighting for. Bolotnikov did his best to keep their spirits high. He meted out severe punishment, when necessary, or stood before his army, offering himself in sacrifice to the Cossacks when that was more tactful; however the defenders' patience could be restored for periods that were becoming increasingly shorter. Finally the situation grew so tense that the fighters seized Prince Shakhovskoi who had recklessly promised to produce Tsar Dmitri. The rebels desperately needed the tsar's presence. In this age of popular revolts, the person so badly needed rarely fails not to turn up.

True, it was not easy to raise Tsar Dmitri from the dead a second time. A year had already passed between his death and the "miraculous escape." Aside from Mikhail Molchanov taking the role once, nothing indicates any sound basis for the belief in his existence. Who was then the person who stepped into the shoes of the first impostor? How did he get to Starodub of all places? On this issue our sources are rather hazy. This is due to the fact that, because of his colorful nature, these pass on much gossip about him, but none reveal his origins, since everybody was certain that the new, the second false tsar was an impostor. A fraud even in his capacity of false tsar. A fake false tsar.

It is again Konrad Bussow who provides most details on this man. According to him, Molchanov and Mniszech had something to do with the affair, and the new candidate hesitated long before accepting their offer. He found the venture so uncertain and dangerous that he crossed the Russian frontier in the company of a Polish nobleman, Miechowicki, without "unveiling" himself. Content at first with the lesser lie, he posed as a royal relative, a descendant of the Nagoy clan. He and his followers tried to assess the public mood and spread the news of the impending arrival of Tsar Dmitri. Because of their success, the population far and near was waiting for Dmitri. But the days passed and the long-awaited tsar failed to arrive. Losing their patience, some residents of Starodub thrashed a scribe who served the false Nagoy. They wanted to learn the whereabouts of the man's master. In his desperate predicament the servant now pointed at the false Nagoy: "Fools, can't you see your tsar standing in front of you? He has been here among you for a while, keeping his true identity secret only to test your loyalty!" That was, according to Bussow, the great revelation, supposedly witnessed by a man of the Bolotnikov faction, sent by the Tula leaders to seek Dmitri, whom the mutinous troops were demanding to see.[8]

According to another (Polish) version, the second false Dmitri was a converted Jew serving as a tutor at the house of the Orthodox priest of Moghilev, which he had to quit suddenly after seducing his master's wife. A third version confirms the man's profession as a tutor but dates his hardships from the time he was imprisoned for spying. Beside these three, there are several other explanations concerning the identity of the second false tsar. (Thus one has him as the son of Prince Andrei Kurbsky, once a powerful opponent of Tsar Ivan IV.) Bussow's version still seems to be the most convincing, as it puts the struggle in Russia and the Mniszech clan's financial need in context with the false Dmitri's reemergence.[9]

The Starodub "miracle" gave new hope to the defenders at Tula but ultimately did them more harm than good. The false Dmitri's great move took place in July 1607. By late summer he had managed to gather a small army, and the local population backed him with the same old enthusiasm; yet, he failed to hurry to the aid of his "subjects." Shuisky's army was forced into action by his emergence: they wanted a quick end to the siege before facing the new Dmitri's relief army—if it really came. The besiegers started an enormous project in early August with the aim of building a huge dam on the Tula River so as to flush out the rebels of the fortress. The project succeeded: the rebels were forced to give up their stronghold. They must have succeeded, however, in making some deal, as otherwise it would be difficult to understand why "Tsarevich Peter" and Bolotnikov were executed only some months after the surrender, why the nobles involved in the revolt remained unscathed and why a mass of men were let go free. Shuisky's commander must have found it pressing to make concessions. Then, as his position seemed to be consolidating, Shuisky broke the terms and had the two ringleaders executed.[10]

Tsar Vasily was to be disappointed yet again. The second false Dmitri, receiving the news of the fall of Tula, fled to the district of Komaritskaya which had loyally supported the first. Then, with winter setting in, he moved on to Oryol. Here, however, he was able to go about the undisturbed and organized an army out of Polish and Lithuanian fortune hunters pouring into his camp since the autumn of 1607 and especially in early 1608. This was when King Sigismund III of Poland, crushed a domestic feudal revolt, and the unfortunate Polish nobles now tried their luck across the border. Experienced mercenaries, they considerably boosted the false tsar's self-confidence and military strength. The population in the south and the Cossacks also supported the second false Dmitri. By the spring of 1608, he was already in command of a force of fifteen thousand.

His army was joined by the dispersed remnants of Bolotnikov's revolt. As his launching area and popular base was more or less identical with those of the previous movements, the early seventeenth century social struggle in Russia had reached its third phase with the emergence of the second false Dmitri. This phase, however, was different from the previous ones in two important aspects. First, the earlier phases had at times born the distinct mark of pure social conflicts and this character was lost now. Second, the influence of foreign powers on the power struggle in Russia had not been as considerable as it was now.

This special feature highlights the personal qualities of those who headed the broad social resistance in its different phases. On the surface, of course, there was always one name, "Tsar Dmitri," spearheading the insurgents against the lawful tsar's authority. But the characters and goals of the individuals assuming that name were not at all the same. Grishka Otrepiev, the first false tsar, was undoubtedly a self-possessed individual who was able to maintain the integrity of both himself and his country and could make people really believe that he was the tsar. As one of the leaders of the mass movement, acting in the name of the first false Dmitri, Bolotnikov gave the resistance movement an image of social struggle and remained the champion of the downtrodden right until he died on the rack.

Compared to these two remarkable individuals, the second false tsar was a petty impostor. It is no accident that his contemporaries referred to him simply as "the felon." Even his followers regarded him as "extremely impudent and rude," and the Poles maintained that he took orders from his escort Miechowicki. While his principals were later to change frequently, the fact remained that the second false Dmitri was a puppet of his Polish-Lithuanian masters all along. His charismatic name, however, ensured mass support, and there is no doubt that the fake false tsar endeavored to meet expectations as much as he could, promising freedom to every serf and slave as well as "rewards hard to imagine." However, he stumbled in his role as soon as a few thousand Cossacks arrived to his camp, led by a certain Fedor Fedorovich, yet another false tsarevich who claimed to be "Tsarevich Peter's" brother. The new Dmitri found it too hard to tolerate the rivalry of another obvious impostor and sent him away, even at the cost of weakening his own army.

True, he did not miss those troops for the moment. In a battle on April 30, 1608, he defeated the tsar's brother, Dmitri Shuisky and found the road to Moscow wide open. Early in the summer he made camp at Tushino, a small village near the capital, and prepared for the decisive assault. He was not to know he would wait in vain for a year and a half here. The Shuisky camp was still far from being so weak as to allow him to take the town in a single gulp. The false tsar's army grew even larger through the arrival of another seven thousand Poles led by Jan Petr Sapieha, enabling the pretender to set up court in Tushino and to attempt to encircle Moscow bringing the area around the capital under his own jurisdiction.

This new situation demanded that Tushino be turned into a fortified settlement and second capital. It was surrounded by trenches and mounds. The "tsar's" residence was erected, followed by those of the nobility. Administration buildings were put up next. All in all, the false tsar created here a small and distorted copy of the country's official capital. He had a Boyar Duma and appropriately staffed government offices. He named new boyars, appointed governors to the newly-taken towns, rewarded people with land, held court and passed verdicts. As a capital, Tushino obviously lacked much. It became far too small for its function, it was soon enfolded in such an amount of filth and odor that, according to contemporary sources, life was hardly bearable there. The false tsar's attempt to act as a real ruler might be considered humorous or even a parody if it had not been so serious. His "court" was adorned by a number of dignitaries: in a power struggle whose outcome had grown uncertain, every aristocratic family found it necessary to "delegate" at least one member to the "Tushino capital" as well, in a down-to-earth instinct of "you never know what tomorrow will bring." Later even a genuine archbishop arrived (as prisoner) at the camp. He was quickly made patriarch and thus bore his Tushino hardships rather proudly. Years later he would have vastly different memories of his months spent here. He did not even like to recall being made an archbishop by a false tsar (the first), which is no wonder considering the fact that he was Filaret of the Romanov clan, father of the first Romanov tsar.[11]

The second false tsar's legitimacy was provided by a woman rather than by the patriarch. For a short time before widowhood, Marina Mniszech had been the first false tsar's wife, and she confirmed the identity of the second false tsar of Tushino as her husband.

That was an unexpected announcement. Marina, the undersized Catholic, last appeared in our story when the outraged people of Moscow mounted a pogrom against the Poles following "Tsar Dmitri's" death. The tsarina, however, survived the mob's lynching mood (according to some reports, she hid under a lady-in-waiting's petticoat) and, together with her father and many retainers, was first detained, then exiled. Two years had passed since then—and two years is an extremely long time for a woman as ambitious as Marina was. International politics, however, played into her hands. Shuisky made an agreement with the Polish king to set Polish prisoners free under the condition that they were to be called back to Poland. Actually, King Sigismund III would have ordered them back in vain, since most of the Poles fighting in Russia had fled there to avoid his revenge. Shuisky in turn only invited trouble by letting Mniszech and his companions go.

It is impossible today to trace her route. Shortly after being freed, however, the former tsarina was not within the bounds of the Kingdom of Poland and Lithuania but at the court of the second false Dmitri. She was taken prisoner by a special raiding force of the new false tsar, although a more likely version is that Voevoda Mniszech allowed himself to be caught, so that he could sell his daughter a second time. Her price had dropped in the meantime, for she was now worth only 300,000 gold ducats and the Seversk region. Nevertheless, assessments of the bargain differed. Even in false Dmitri's camp many people had reservations about, not the idea, but the doubtful outcome. Everyone understood how important it was for the second impostor tsar to be recognized by the first impostor's wife but it was not at all sure that Marina would agree. Indeed, when Marina Mniszech had her first view of "her long-awaited spouse," the new candidate husband's extreme ugliness upset her so much that, according to one eyewitness, she raised her dagger, crying, "I'd rather die!" After being pacified, she consented to the transaction. As she would admit later, it was impossible for her now to return to Poland as a mere noblewoman. She still regarded herself as a tsarina, and her only chance of being restored to her "rights" was through the "felon of Tushino," the man whose looks as well as character disgusted her. By recognizing him, she produced a trump for strengthening the second false Dmitri's position in the eyes of the outside world. (As for herself, she only shared a bed with the false tsar she recognized as her husband, after she secretly married him "again.")[12] By the autumn of 1608, dual power had been established in every respect in Russia. Tushino was the stronger pole during this period: exploiting the entrenched nature of the war outside Moscow, the false tsar's raiding forces had the larger half of the country swear fealty to their lord. At first the population supported the "real" tsar. Yet, they were soon to realize that he was far from being the redeemer they had expected. His Cossacks and Poles looted peaceful estates without restraint; what is more, the latter even abused the "true faith."

The impostor had thus become such a genuine tsar that popular resistance against his authority started—fittingly—under the rules of the false-tsar belief. In the year 1608, a score of new false tsareviches emerged. A man called Ivan-August declared himself to be Ivan IV's son. A certain Lavrenty was held to be identical with the neverborn child of Tsarevich Ivan. And the false Tsareviches Peter, Fedor, Klementy, Savely, Semyon, Vasily, Yerofey, Gavrila and Martin came forward as Tsar Fedor's sons. Even a revolt that broke out in the town of Astrakhan could not have done so without false tsareviches. There were two of them here: Osinovik stepped forward as Tsarevich Ivan and Lavrenty as Tsar Fedor's son. These false tsareviches carried so little weight that almost no information survives on them. Nevertheless, the simultaneous emergence in such numbers beautifully illustrates the inflation of the false-tsar doctrine. Through his personality and deeds the second false Dmitri had so corrupted the method that almost every self-reliant host of Cossacks had the courage to try their luck with a false tsar of its own. Mostly they turned against the felon of Tushino, who was everything but loyal to his royal kin. He circulated letters of denunciation in the country, claiming to be "the only" rightful ruler and maintaining, for instance, that Tsar Fedor had never had sons. He even put a reward on their heads, threatening to have them scourged and actually executed two of them.[13]

Unlike the rival false tsareviches, a far more serious danger to him was posed by Prince Mikhail Skopin-Shuisky, Tsar Vasily's nephew who gathered in Novgorod an army of the residents of the towns north of the Volga with a large number of auxiliary forces from Sweden. After an extended period spent in organizing itself, his army set off to relieve Moscow in the spring of 1609, though not in any great haste; late in the summer they had not yet arrived near the capital. The coming of the autumn, however, brought decisive changes in Russia. Judging the situation to be ripe for his intervention, Sigismund besieged Smolensk. Interestingly, this had a positive effect on Shuisky's situation, as the Polish king ordered his subjects (that is, those who obeyed him) to return from the false tsar's camp. This, together with news of the approach of Skopin-Shuisky, put an end to the year and a half of the Tushino camp. Afraid that his followers might hand him over to Sigismund III, the "felon" ran to the fortress of Kaluga to await a turn in his fortune.[14]

His assumption seemed to be proved right when in July 1610, despite vast superiority in numbers, the tsar's army was unexpectedly defeated by a Polish force sent from Smolensk. The false tsar thought his time had come, for the roads to Moscow were now undefended. But the Poles had also realized this and, soon there were two armies; the Polish Chief Hetman Stanislas Zólkiewski's and the false tsar's, marching against Moscow along two different routes. This turn of events triggered off a resounding reaction in Moscow. In an unprecedented development Tsar Vasily Shuisky was forced to abdicate, and a small group of boyars took control. They pondered which was the lesser of two evils and, deciding the Poles to be less dangerous, invited them to the city on condition that they would help them drive off the false tsar. That posed no problem. The Poles beat the impostor back from under the walls of Moscow and remained in the Kremlin, which they did not leave for the next two years.[15]

The false-tsar belief must have sunk low if Russian aristocrats of the "true faith" preferred heretic "Latin believers" to it. The Tushino reign of the figurehead false tsar, allegedly manipulated by foreigners, brought destruction and anarchy to Russia, which is why most of society turned from him. Those who remained with him were one or two Polish fortune hunters and a few thousand Cossacks. By this time his role had become that of a leader of Cossack robbers and looters. His name put fear into the hearts of the Moscow nobility: no rebellion was renowned for its sentimentality. All the moral polish was gone from the false tsar's movement now. The boyars' choice in inviting the Poles is explained by obvious class interests, but by doing so, they submitted themselves to a foreign power and tolerated it in mute discipline as long as a new emergence of the false tsar threatened.

A rather peculiar situation unfolded over the next few months: a few thousand foreign mercenaries, holed up in the Kremlin, kept the city of one hundred thousands in check and even kept the road between the Russian capital and the faraway Polish border open. The false-tsar movement was hindered by the upsurge of a struggle for national liberation from the Poles. Beginning with the emergence of the second false Dmitri, the belief in false tsars was gradually losing ground, becoming a burden for the overwhelming majority of the religious ethnic Russians living within the empire's borders. The days of the "felon of Tushino" were petering out. Thus it was quite insignificant that one of his trusted followers, a Tartar named Petr Urusov, killed him to revenge an old family feud on December 11, 1610.[16]

Now was the time for the struggle against the foreigners, especially the Poles, to take priority; it was this that unified the nation at last. The belief in false tsars lost its ideological role. Although the Cossacks tried to bring back the three-times-dead Tsarevich Dmitri a fourth time, they failed. The story can be told briefly.

A former Muscovite student called Sidorka (or Matyushka) assumed Dmitri's name in Ivangorod, in March 1611. Hearing the news, the Cossacks of Pskov swarmed to him like bees to honey, and soon the whole town had taken his side. Nevertheless, he had only a local following until a fatal breach occurred in the ranks of the "first popular uprising," the broad alliance of serving nobles and Cossacks bent on liberating Moscow.[17] What happened was that, before managing to retake the town from the Poles, the Cossacks drove away their own allies but then failed to complete the siege by themselves. Meanwhile Smolensk was taken by the Poles and Novgorod by the Swedes; there was a garrison of foreign troops in the Kremlin, and the country was being looted by both foreign mercenaries and Cossack raiding parties.

A new declaration of a struggle for liberation was then made in Nizhny-Novgorod by the towns along and north of the Volga under the leadership of serving nobles. In the parts of the country that were still in Russian hands, this movement, known as the "'second popular uprising," slowly gained ground over the Cossack remnants (still under Moscow) of the "first popular uprising." To regain their leading position, the Cossacks tried the false-tsar trick again and swore fealty to the third false Dmitri, that is Sidorka, in March 1612. Their hopes were disappointed, though; even such traditional bases for any false tsar as the townships of Tula and Kaluga refused to recognize the new false tsar. Thus the third false Dmitri not only failed to improve the Cossacks' position but even removed a considerable part of their previous following. All the Cossacks could do now was make a pact with the service gentry and city dwellers led by Kuzma Minin and Prince Dmitri Pozharsky, and a precondition for that pact was the removal of the false tsar. For that purpose, a representative of the Cossacks went to Pskov and unveiled the impostor. The last hurdle in the way of the new alliance was now gone, and this "second popular uprising" succeeded in its goal when Moscow was liberated in October 1612.[18]

The following year the first Romanov tsar was crowned. It might be thought that this was the end of the period in Russian history so rightfully called the Time of Troubles by contemporary sources. In fact, there was still long way to go towards a real consolidation, for it was hindered for years by yet another false tsarevich. This new threat to consolidation was not a simple false tsarevich but one doubly or even three times false. Dangerous to the whole country, the new adversary was none other than Marina Mniszech's son by the felon of Tushino, a child whom contemporaries simply referred to as "the little felon." His mother, of course, had no scruples over the affair: she considered the child to be the real, genuine Dmitri's son, that is, Ivan IV's only grandson and thus the rightful heir to the throne. Since the Romanovs could claim to be relatives of the last legitimate tsar only on the maternal side, the claim of "Tsarevich Ivan" to the throne caused serious trouble even at Tsar Michael's election. The regime therefore mobilized great forces to arrest Marina together with her child and her new confidant, Hatman Ivan Zarutsky of the Cossacks (who, according to some sources, had once also pretended to be Tsar Dmitri) and disperse their forces. This was successfully done near the far-off town of Astrakhan. The latest false Dmitri (fourth or fifth; we cannot tell for sure, as in the meantime somebody else also had assumed the name in Astrakhan) died on the stake. Marina's little boy was hanged, and the twice tsarina was sent to a nunnery. The great upheavals had ended; the country slowly began to pull itself back to order. In the new historical situation, a false-tsar ideology outlived its usefulness; the very concept had became a stumbling block to consolidation. Thus the annihilation of the little felon, however brutally it was done, served the interest of society as a whole.[19]

Chapter 4

IMPOSTORS ABROAD

From the year 1613 on, Russia had a tsar again, even if he was an adolescent never far from his mother's skirt. But with its self-appointed, killed or abdicated tsars, with the boyars who had made a pact with the Catholic enemy and with slaves and serfs in revolt against their masters, the preceding decade of the Time of Troubles had demoralized society so much that now, after over two years without a tsar, everybody breathed a sigh of relief. There were still enormous chunks of territory in the possession of foreign powers. Polish mercenaries were still on the rampage, and even the leaderless Cossack raiding parties did not spare a population that had long wished to be left to live in peace. Then a powerful neighbor hungry for booty, the Kingdom of Poland and Lithuania, reappeared, and Prince Wladislaw's determined onslaught had to be beaten back by an army. By the end of the decade, however, Russia had managed to normalize its relations with the Swedes and Poles and could thus begin to treat its war wounds. A host of both minor and major reform measures were taken in the organization of the army, in the state administration, in taxation; Russian society was slowly returning to normalcy. Long past were the days when people rushed heedlessly to one or another new false tsarevich's banner to help shake the establishment. Now they were longing for that same establishment and cursed themselves for having allowed themselves to be taken in by a few impostors.[1] This is why the decades following the troublesome period were not fruitful for the false-tsar belief. The government itself also did its best by having "the little felon," the second false Dmitri's young son, executed. Not content with the false tsar's death, his son was killed in order to close the file on the false Dmitris, once and for all. Nevertheless, with our knowledge of the consistency of the false-tsar idea, we should not be surprised to learn that, less than three decades after the death of Ivan, the false tsar's doubly false tsarevich son and three new false tsars emerged at the same time. All three of them preferred to be reborn outside Russia.

Of one of them we know next to nothing, not even precisely when he made his appearance on the scene: it must have happened sometime between 1639 to 1643. The hospodar of Moldavia, eager to please the Moscow government, had the false tsarevich "Ivan Dmitrievich" arrested and sent his skull and hide to Moscow. The tsar appreciated such a gesture of neighborly civility and, by return of ambassador, sent back the ill-fated false-little-felon's skin, stuffed with gold and all kinds of precious stones.[2]

A harder task fell to those representing Moscow who left in 1643 for Poland and had, among other important business, to complain in secret negotiations to King Wladislaw of the granting of haven to another two false tsareviches. According to the Russians' information, one of them had the stigma on his back and had been staying for the last fifteen years at a Jesuit monastery in Brest-Litovsk. Polish negotiators at first tried to deny the importance of the matter. They said yes, there was a nobleman's servant, a scribe whom his fellow servants mockingly called tsarevich; but how could anyone think that the pans of Poland took such a clown seriously? Yet the boyars stood their ground and demanded that the "clown" be handed over to them. So in the next round of talks the Poles had to supply a more detailed explanation, the essence of which was that "Ivan Dmitrievich" is really a Pole, they said, and one of his compatriots claimed that he was a tsarevich back in his childhood. Sigismund III did in fact supply him with an annual allowance. But, according to the negotiators passing on their king's reply, the two countries were at war with each other at that time.

As soon as the "eternal peace" was signed, the false tsarevich was dropped.[3]

As the above exchange shows, the international situation had radically changed since the heyday of the false Dmitries. Now Russia was the stronger of the neighbors, and the Poles were more interested in reaching an agreement. However, they did not want to yield completely even in this matter. They suggested interrogating the man in the boyars' presence. As a matter of fact, the man said he was Ivan Luba, son of Dmitri Luba, who took him to Russia during the Time of Troubles. Dmitri was killed during the fighting, and one of his comrades, a certain Belinsky, took the orphan along with him, telling everyone that the child had been trusted to him by the mother, the false tsarina Marina Mniszech. When the child had become older, his "guardian" took his case to the Seym, the parliament of Poland, and managed to get Sigismund III to provide him with six thousand gold ducats per year. The boy was sent to the Semyonovsky monastery in Brest-Litovsk to learn Russian, Polish and Latin. But when peace was concluded with the Russians, his allowance shrank to one hundred ducats; finally after the "eternal peace" was signed, he was completely forgotten. Poor Luba now turned to Belinsky and asked who he really was. Belinsky told him that he was Luba's son and the intention had been to swap him with the real "little felon" before the latter's execution. The plotters had been tardy, and so he did not die for the other boy; he had still been useful as his replacement. Therein lay the seed of the idea of making him "Tsar Dmitri's" son.[4]

The Russian envoys were not content with merely exploring this story of a sad life. Though the Poles were ready to sign a document to the effect that Luba would not come forward as a tsarevich in their country, the boyars also wanted guarantees to prevent that from happening outside the Polish-Lithuanian border; for this reason they still considered having the Polish nobleman and former unwilling false tsarevich extradited to Russia as the safest solution. This was all very well but the rather wide-ranging rights of the nobility in the Kingdom prohibited that. The pans of Poland therefore suggested at first turning Luba from worldly pleasures and making a monk out of him; they then would have agreed even to have him locked up for as long as the Russians desired. The Russian envoys proved to be stubborn and made all further negotiation pending on the outcome of this matter. When the Polish delegation left for Moscow at the end of the following year, it took Jan (Ivan) Luba along. A lucky turn of fortune for the false tsarevich of Polish origin was provided by an event painful for the Russians: the death of Tsar Michael. In this (internationally always delicate) situation the boyars accepted a compromise and allowed Luba to be taken home and kept under watch in Poland. The nobleman himself was indeed innocent: he could not help being made a false tsarevich in his childhood. Although he was able to return home in peace, it seems that no false tsarevich lived to die in old age. Two years after his return from Moscow, Luba was killed during a Tartar raid in Poland.[5]

Not even half a year after the Luba episode Russian envoys relayed alarming news from Kaffa, another false Tsarevich Ivan was on the loose. A certain Archimandrita (abbot) Joakhim reported being approached in the Crimea by a man claiming to be Tsar Dmitri's son who asked him to go to Kaluga with a letter that would make people stand behind him. Those sent to gather intelligence were quick to do so: they soon found a Ukrainian Cossack prisoner who had known the new false Ivan. This impostor turned out to be a certain Ivashka Vergunyonok who, after being driven out by his mother, had gone into service with the Cossack who reported him. A year later he went on to the northern Donets area, then spent a year on the Don where he was frequently set up for trying to make a living through robbery. So, in a company of four, he moved on to the steppe, the no man's land, where he was taken prisoner by the Tartars. They in turn sold him to a Jew at Kaffa. There he put on his act: he "revealed" to his master that he was the Moscow ruler's son, and from that time on his master treated him with much respect. To be on the safe side, the new tsarevich even produced proof of his identity: he had a local Russian woman brand his back with a star and crescent. Then he started showing the branding to his fellow slaves and promised to distribute huge prizes to them as soon as he got his throne back. The Russians believed him and delivered food and drink to the Jew's household for three years.

In Vergunyonok's case we can see a petty version of the false-tsarevich tale. Here it was used to get good wine and food; perhaps even a partnership was formed by Ivashka and his master. So the news could hardly have been welcome that the khan of the Crimea, having got wind of the rumors on his identity, had Ivashka brought before him. At his court, the khan had him taken care of by Jews again as he lived under close supervision. From here he was taken to the grand vizier's court in Constantinople with the purpose of using him, if necessary, as a bargaining chip in diplomatic skirmishes with the Russians. Of course, those who had eyes saw that he was a very last men to be used as a diplomatic trump; accordingly he was set free soon. However, his drunken conduct and a brawl with some Muslims took him straight to prison.[6]

The Cossack lad who was willing to do anything for a drink, even act as a false tsar, becoming superfluous to the grand vizier who had several irons in the fire. At the time there was already another false tsarevich at his court, evidently more suitable for the role.

Actually, the grand vizier could not immediately choose between the two. His initial mistrust concerning the second false tsarevich was caused by the fact that, in confrontation with the Russian envoys, the impostor looked less than thirty years old; the Russians kept maintaining that Tsar Vasily Shuisky whom the man was claiming to be a son of, had been dead for about forty years. (This, by the way, was not true.) Under the weight of this "proof," the grand vizier conceded that "this is a cunning man and says many false things but the other one who has come from the Crimea is really a genuine tsarevich." But as it soon turned out that the tale of Ivashka with the decorated back was even more transparent, the false Shuisky returned to the fore of events.[7]

In a letter to the vizier (it was translated by an Orthodox priest who immediately informed the Russian envoys) this man described the following events: he was half a year old when his father, Vasily Shuisky, was dragged off to Polish-Lithuanian territory; but the writer, his son, was given to loyal people to be taken care of. Then, when Tsar Michael took the throne, he called the child to Moscow and presented him with part of the duchy of Perm. The young man became bored with life in this desolate region and returned to the capital where he was detained. His former guardians again came to his rescue and secured his release. He found his way to Moldavia, but the hospodar robbed him there, taking even his father's gem-studded cross off him, and almost meted out the same fate to him as befell his brother who was skinned on his orders.

Thus the false Shuisky knew the story of the false tsarevich executed in Moldavia and cleverly tried to enhance the credibility of his own with that episode. It certainly cannot be said that he was lacking in tactical sense. He asked the sultan for troops to be able to go to the Russian border, vehemently claiming that the local population would not resist him. He promised Astrakhan, as a reward to the Turks, an area they had long wanted. At the time the Turks had neither the will nor the interest to go to war with the Russia; the grand vizier wisely kept silent on hearing the offer. Later, on receiving information of unrest among the Cossacks, the porte regarded the false tsarevich as a useful card to play in the international game. In the end, however, the Turkish councilor of state lost his diplomatic gamble, which meant the silk cord for him. Nobody there needed the false Shuisky any more, so he ran away and returned to Moldavia where his luck again deserted him; he was caught and returned to Constantinople. There he escaped severe punishment only by donning a turban and converting to the Muslim faith. At the first opportunity, however, he dressed as a Greek and escaped but was caught again. This time he was unable to escape being circumcised. His life was spared, however, and was held in strict custody.[8]

For over three years he disappeared from the pages of Russian sources. The Muscovites did not know that in the meantime he had been to Bulgaria and Serbia, had gone on to Venice and Rome to try his fortune. In the Vatican he did not hesitate to ask for the pope's help or to change religions again; naturally this time he converted to Catholicism and even promised that, should he be successful in his quest, he would turn his entire country to the Catholic faith. During his stay in Rome he spoke of his life, putting an emphasis on his sufferings as a prisoner of the heathen Turks and this obviously served him well here. Nevertheless, the credibility of his story suffered much because of his habit of changing his name. Once he introduced himself as Vladimir Yoann Timofey, on another occasion as Yoann Timofey Vladimir Shuisky and yet on another occasion treating the genealogy of the Russian tsars with some nonchalance, he said he was the "great-grandson of the Moscow Emperors Fedor and Dmitri, son of the Great Emperor Vasily." In Vatican documents he is featured in a longer version as Giovanni Timotei Vladimirski Sciuiski Moskovski, in a shorter version as Gion Sciuiski. Although the pope thus had no idea who his guest actually was, this did not seem to concern him at all. The Moscow government had no information on all this, but it did know exactly whom it was dealing with in the guise of the new false tsar.[9]

He had been identified already in Constantinople by a Russian embassy scribe who—how small the world was even then!—had been a fellow clerk with the false tsarevich in a Moscow government office. As it turned out, our man's real name was Timoshka Akundinov. His father was a *strelets*. He had left the country after a "memorable" deed: he had set his house on fire—with his wife inside. The evidence supplied by his former colleague produced some surprising details. It became clear that Akundinov was the very person about whom, along with "Ivan" Luba, the Russians had complained angrily to the Poles that for four years there was someone living in the kingdom who had claimed to be Semion Shuisky. According to their information, the impostor had arrived from the Ukraine and found employment with an Orthodox priest who, noticing the "mark" on his back, had sent him to his superior who in turn had sent him even higher; finally, the Seym itself voted to provide for him at the government's expense. In 1643 the Poles allaid Russian concerns by informing Moscow that, on learning of his fraud, they had horse whipped the false tsarevich and had driven him away. True, Akundinov's next appearance was recorded in Moldavia.[10]

Nevertheless, in 1649 he was again very close to the scenes of his early wanderings. After a totally unfruitful stay of four months in Rome, he returned again via Austria, Hungary and Poland to the Ukrainian Cossacks. Here he was found by the tsar's people who tried to induce him to go home. Interestingly, even Akundinov himself pondered a return home and was thus restrained about his royal ancestry. First of all he declared that he did not regard himself either as tsar or tsarevich; he was simply a grandson of Tsar Vasily Shuisky. Then he tried to find favor with the tsar by saying that many rulers had called him to their courts but he wanted to serve only Tsar Alexis because the Orthodox faith was sacrosanct to him. He made this declaration in writing and sent it to the governor of Putivl, Prince Ivan Prozorovsky. His very humble though well-written letter discloses a skilled demagogue to those who read it at such a distance in time: "In a foreign land, living in the unknown, my rootlessness binds me," he writes, "and though I am not chained, I can hardly breathe." At the same time, he offered the tsar "the key to my heart" simply to soften the autocrat's heart towards him. The former clerk regarded it as especially important to ask that his papers not be filed away. In order to demonstrate his goodwill, he swore not to reveal "his secret" to anybody around him. This epistle that played on the chords of sentiment was answered by the prince at Putivl with a rather prosaic directness: "Come to Putivl without delay!" However, his country's hospitality was not that important Timoshka, so he stayed put. Instead of going, he complained with reason that the Russians were sending too many people "to view" him and even threw a theatrical tantrum because they did not believe him.[11]

Then Moscow turned to the chief hetman of the Ukraine, Bogdan Khmelnitsky. He rejected the Russian demand, referring to the "Cossack freedom" which forbade the extradition of anyone who fled to them. Since the Ukrainian Cossacks could not risk arousing Russian anger at them as they were at war with Poland at that moment, Khmelnitsky later promised to hand Akundinov over to Moscow when he was found. Thus he granted a little time for the false tsarevich, who found himself in an increasingly tight corner; he therefore made another attempt to come to an agreement with his compatriots. During his encounter with Unkovsky, the tsar's envoy, he went even further in modesty: "If I am called the son of Vasily Ivanovich, I do not call myself that, they call me that here...but in reality I am his daughter's son," he admitted. He thus practically renounced his status of a false tsarevich, assured the tsar of his full loyalty and obviously wished only to be able to withdraw with honor. But even that was too much for the tsar's administration. Unkovsky made it clear to Akundinov that he could not guarantee him safe conduct home. He even tried to hire assassins to have him killed.[12]

Akundinov had to move again. This time he fled to Hungary. From there he set out for Sweden with a safe pass provided by Prince George Rákóczi of Transylvania. In 1651 Moscow learned the alarming news from Sweden of the false Shuisky's reappearance. The Russian authorities now launched an operation more extensive than ever before. While putting diplomatic pressure on the queen of Sweden, they seized on foreign territory the false tsarevich's closest confidant and followed Akundinov from the capital to Narva and on to Revel where finally they captured him. The local governor, however, came to his rescue, and Akundinov managed to escape. All the same, he had to leave Sweden. The tsar's men, however, never allowed him to slip away from them, tailing him ceaselessly, appearing on his heels in Lubeck and

Brandenburg. Finally they caught up with him in Holstein. This was the last stage of the first false Shuisky's long pilgrimage; Prince Friedrich exchanged him for a Russian charter granting him trade with Persia.[13]

By that time Akundinov's loyal companion, Kostka Koniyuhovsky, had long been in Moscow. Under terrible torture he confessed his master's deeds. Thus it turned out that, at first in Lithuania, Timoshka had pretended to be a certain Ivan Karazeisky, voevoda of Vologda and governor of Perm. He had assumed Shuisky's name only in Constantinople under the spell of evil Lithuanian books on astrology. He had a seal made for himself in Rome and got to Sweden after the intervention of his Ukrainian friend Vigovsky with Prince Rákóczi. Kostka concluded his confession by saying that in Sweden Timoshka had converted to the Lutheran faith.

Kostka Koniyuhovsky's statements are exact indicators of the limits of human courage. In the first round he said only what was absolutely necessary, giving up only as much incriminating information as his inquisitors already knew. Of course, he tried to clear himself of all involvement. After being racked three times and enduring fifteen lashes, he still did not add anything. A few days later he was worked over again. This time Kostka confessed that Akundinov had wanted to march with the Turks against Astrakhan. After another sixteen lashings and being scalded twice, he still said the same. Four days later he remembered his master wanting to contact the rebels of Pskov. At last the authorities no longer wanted to learn more from him, though he would have confessed to anything by now.[14]

On December 8, 1653, the false Tsar Semyon Shuisky himself took Kostka's place in the torture chamber. He had known what had been awaiting him. After his arrest he had tried to commit suicide by jumping off the cart and rolling under the wheels—in vain. Once in Moscow, he confessed. He said he had been left an orphan as a small child. The archbishop of Vologda had said in admiration of his sharp mind that he was a descendant of princes.

He had escaped to Lithuania in fear after his paternal benefactor, the chief clerk Patrikeyev, lost favor. It had been his father who had called him Shuisky. Later his mother was brought out of a nunnery and stood before him. She looked at him and said, "This is my son Timoshka." Akundinov remained silent for a long time, then asked, "What is your name?" Then he said, "This nun is not my mother but her sister. She was good to me, a mother to me." Now the inquisitors asked the mother again and she repeated, "This is my son Timoshka. I gave birth to him in Vologda thirty-six years ago." "Then Timoshka was quartered," the contemporary source concludes dryly.[15]

What was behind the reported confrontation between mother and son? Who told the truth and who lied? Was the elderly nun responsible for her son's death? These are questions left without answer in the laconic official documents. Still, the unsentimental records of a torture session could help the modern psychohistorian. Perhaps the ill-fated Kostka gives us the answer in his statement on his friend's youth. His account reveals a terrible family tragedy. The contemporary document has a dramatic force:

> When (Timoshka's mother) remarried, Timoshka quarreled with many people and then, angry with his mother, started thinking on how to run away to Lithuania...And on the night that he took to flight, Timoshka took his daughter and son over to Ivan Peskov's yard and then set his house and wife on fire....[16]

A crime story on the pages of a yellowed document from the seventeenth century. Why did Timoshka do his deed? In his bitterness over his mother's new marriage? But then, why was it his wife whom he killed? Did he think she had something to do with it? The answer to this we are not likely to learn now. One point is clear, however: Timofey Akundinov was close to his mother. He demonstrated that during the interrogation when he admitted everything but refused to recognize his mother in order to save her from any ensuing trouble. Yet he could not help saying, since it was their last encounter in life, how much he owed to the woman standing before him.

Akundinov was not a typical criminal. He was a murderer who may have wanted so much to return home because after many years he wanted to see his children again. He was far too resourceful and vain to flee from justice merely as a common criminal. The nocturnal arsonist was made into a false tsar by an act of fate. His intelligence, coupled with his political and tactical instinct, made a fine performance of his role possible. In many aspects he resembled the first false Dmitri. Yet, his life as a false tsarevich was a constant running of the gauntlet. His story well illustrates the enormous changes taking place in Europe, including Russia, in the decades that followed the Time of Troubles; change for the worse for those fishing in troubled waters.

Of the four false tsareviches who appeared after 1613, none claimed to be false Dmitri, which shows that the impostors assuming that name had discredited forever the belief in Dmitri the redeemer. Although three more attempts occurred to extend, as it were, the life of the legend by abusing the name of the second false Dmitri's son for their purposes, these took place beyond Russia's borders, without any echo in Russia itself. Timoshka Akundinov emerged by assuming the identity of another—lawful—tsar's son, although his attempt was all the more futile since Shuisky was an extremely unpopular and unimportant tsar in the eyes of his Russian subjects. From the above events we can draw the conclusion that the false-tsar belief gradually waned and lost its popular base. In the mid-seventeenth century the plague of rebellions that swept a number of Russian towns was no longer inspired by an ideology of false tsars; that had by then been replaced by a popular superstition based on the traditional "good tsar—evil boyars" contrast.[17] Another half century had to pass before the myth of a false tsar drew huge crowds again to the camp of a popular leader. But that leader happened to be Stepan Razin.

Chapter 5

THE COSSACK LEADER AND THE INVISIBLE FALSE TSAREVICH

In the half century that followed the coronation of the first Romanov tsar, no false tsars were to trouble Russia. The main reason for this was that self-appointed rulers and anarchy had become more or less identical in the public mind and, after so much restlessness and warfare, all sections of Russian society—except for the Cossacks—wanted, peace. Stability was therefore what the whole society wanted, although it cannot be said that consolidation was automatically followed by a strengthening of the power of the tsar. In the circumstances that prevailed in the Russia of the period, the tsar was by nature a trustee of order:.the greater his power, the stronger his realm. Yet the Time of Troubles had obviously had an impact on the minds of his subjects and thus had their effect on how the following decades developed. At least in that the belief in the omnipotence of the tsar's power was shaken, new strata of society played a part in international affairs and participation in politics became a general demand.

The first half of the seventeenth century is therefore a special chapter in the history of autocracy in Russia. Even the event with which it opened was special, for one of the persons who helped the new tsar to take his throne was Kuzma Minin, a simple fishmonger and butcher. The council meeting on a case-by-case basis, the Zemsky Sobor, also gained a considerable role and relatively broad representation. And it was impossible to keep it secret from the sovereign's immediate and wider entourage that, rather than Michael Romanov (1613–1645), it was actually his father, the Patriarch Filaret, who ruled the country. So there was a weak tsar, and there were relatively broad strata of society that had already gained a taste for political decision-making and wanted to share in decisions again. The consolidation of centralized power thus inevitably bred conflicts.[1]

Indeed, we can go further: contemporaries labeled the whole century as "rebellious." In the first year of the reign of Alexis, Michael's son, autocracy seemed just to be on the verge of success when it was simultaneously attacked on several fronts. One of these attacks initially seemed benign. Beginning with the 1630s growing number of learned monks came to Moscow from the Ukraine and soon made the discovery that certain details in church books and liturgy in Moscow were different from the ones they were familiar with. Since the shaping of close ties with the Ukraine was at that time a favored policy, an ideology now seemed to be provided—namely, the unification of the Orthodox Church, which was in theory one and indivisible but in practice multicephalous. What was a narrow problem of Church policy at first glance polarized society into supporters and opponents of the reforms. In a few years the Orthodox Church in Russia fell apart into an official (reformed) church and a persecuted orthodox (or heretic) church. The two parties fell upon each other with fanaticism, neither asking for nor granting mercy in a holy war. Tens of thousands voluntarily (in groups) chose to die on the pyre rather than to have to address the Lord with three fingers overnight instead of in the old fashion of crossing themselves with only two fingers. Beyond the fact that, for such, these novelties were not secondary nuances of rituals but a deeply felt insult to God. Something else was being demonstrated through this guarding of tradition. In the fluid situation in which values were generally being loosened and morals relaxed, the only solid ground under one's feet was the belief in the immutability of the past. Now, with church reform becoming government policy, religious opposition also became an expression for social discontent.[2]

The Russian Schism removed a considerable segment of the masses from fealty to the central power. What is more, by paying such a high price to have the Church modernized, the government also had to confront the patriarch, who at the apex of the church hierarchy wished to place his person and office over the secular power. Patriarch Nikon, who mercilessly pushed the church reforms through, wanted to elevate the practice of Filaret's time to the level of an ideology by declaring the principle of primacy of the church over the tsar. However, since he was not a relative of the sovereign, it soon became evident, despite his having Tsar Alexis Mikhailovich under his influence for some years, that Russian traditions did not tolerate the subordination of secular to ecclesiastic power. Nikon was accordingly defrocked, excommunicated and exiled to a remote northern monastery.[3]

These skirmishes made the tense domestic situation even more problematic. As early as 1648 an uprising occurred in Moscow because of the introduction and withdrawal of a salt tax, when the authorities started collecting this direct tax in arrears. Characteristically, it started with a humble request to the tsar. Only after the sovereign's "cruel retinue" blocked the settlement of the complaint did public anger turn against some prominent boyars. Tsar Alexis had to throw at least one bone to the mob in order to appease it. The mob immediately tore one Pleshtcheyev to pieces, then caught the other main source of its troubles, the fleeing boyar Trakhaniotov, and killed him too. Since the Moscow revolt was followed by similar upheavals in a score of other towns, the authorities had to take measures more thorough than simply making promises and punishing the leaders of the revolt—hence, the introduction of a new code of laws in 1649 (*Ulozhenie*). This indeed brought order to the towns, which was in the towns' interest to some extent. But the order imposed on Russia was heavy and harsh: like peasants, city dwellers were also bound to their place of residence. The population was in effect listed in caste-like groups according to their origin and professions.[4]

On the other hand, the code strengthened the serving nobility's position through a number of privileges that it granted them, thus considerably promoting the stabilization of centralized power. Indeed the organization of repression on a solid foundation was necessary, since those living in towns did not readily agree to accept so great a change in their status. In the year 1662 another, possibly even more dramatic, insurrection erupted in the capital — this time over the unrestrained issue of copper coins. Bad money sent prices soaring in a situation where tax was demanded in silver coin. Gathered in large bands, the Muscovites had the town under their control for several days; their fury led to a pogrom against the boyars. Tsar Alexis was at the village of Kolomenskoye just then, so the armed mob marched there to ask him for a relaxation of taxes and the surrender of a few boyars. Cornered, the tsar promised all to gain time; his army arrived and mercilessly crushed the deceived mob.[5]

Bound to the soil, serfs sought a different way to register their protest and chose the most traditional one: voting with their feet. On the vast Russian plains they had every chance in the world to escape and lose themselves. The number of fugitives rose especially sharply during the renewed war (1654–1667) between Russia and Poland. Peasants fled before the increasing pressure of taxes for government and landlord as much as before the ravages of war and military draft. This instinctive resistance was not in the least hopeless, for they were always welcome among the Cossacks. A universally-respected law of the Cossacks prescribed that refuge for fugitives. In the long run, not only did serfs and slaves push the river Cossacks' numbers up (which increased their fighting potential considerably) but also contributed to a sharp social polarization among them.

The "Don host" was a peculiar Cossack "republic," a geographic and political establishment independent of the Russian state, granting equal rights to every adult fighting man just as in the democracies of antiquity. The host's most important problems were settled by the *Krug*, the fully representative general assembly. As a matter of fact, the well-to-do Cossacks, the "house owners" were able to manipulate decisions at the expense of their comrades living mostly along the upper section of the Don (commonly called the "naked"). With grants and advantageous trade concessions the Moscow government won the support of the privileged layer of the Cossacks, and through them it exerted its will in the most important matters concerning the outside world. It was all the easier since the Cossacks were not concerned with agriculture or anything other than fishing, hunting and warfare. This meant that economically they were at the absolute mercy of Moscow. By the middle of the century their position was delicate even from the territorial aspect, surrounded as they were on three sides by the Russian realm. Their "normal" relationship with Moscow was nevertheless harmonic, what with the tsar's regularly delivered gifts sent in exchange for their taking up the role of battering ram against the Tartars. This practical alliance between the sovereign and the Cossacks was disrupted only if Cossack forces, out raiding, attacked one or another of Moscow's good neighbors as well and, of course, when the tsar's treasury was entirely empty. The war with Poland was such a case—a situation that made the Don Cossack hives buzz in anger. Their mood was made the worse by the Russian peasants who ran to them to escape serfdom and who were swelling the ranks of "the naked." To make matters more complicated, the Moscow authorities were also casting angry glances at the Don for taking the refugees in and thus actually hindering the implementation of Moscow's policy on bondsmen.[6]

With tsarist donations considerably decreased and delayed, the "naked" Cossacks were literally starving but were unable to set out on plundering raids in the directions of the Azov and the Black Seas. Their route was made difficult by a huge fortress built by the

Turks at Azov, while the Russian forts along the Volga blocked their route towards the Caspian Sea. All that the Cossacks could do was to turn to Moscow and ask for some military employment.

Seven hundred "naked" Cossacks, led by Vasily Us, left for Moscow in the summer of 1666 with the intention of offering their services to the tsar. They stopped at Voronezh and sent two delegations to the capital in quick succession. The trouble was that they did not remain idle until their envoys returned with the (unfavorable) answer. Many of them happened to have been uprooted from that very district, and they were eager to present their bills to their former masters. Their former comrades in misery on the estates quickly joined them. Because of the Cossacks' success in snatching their peasants away and ravaging their lands, panic broke out among the district's landed gentry; they demanded that measures be taken quickly by the government. In consequence, Moscow not only refused the Cossacks' services but even sent an army against them. The Cossacks did not dare risk a battle, and they retreated to the Don. It all seemed to be over.[7]

In fact, it was not at all over. The 1654–1667 Polish war had ended in the meantime, and veteran soldiers arrived on the Don to help consume the food that was in any case insufficient. The "naked army" knew of one way out of their troubles: a looting raid along the Volga all the way to the Caspian Sea. Cossack hosts both large and small kept arriving from the Upper Don to plunder the huge vessels sailing down the wide river. Usually the tsar's troops soon put them to flight; but this situation was to change when a charismatic leader took command of the next raid.

Naturally, the Cossacks had no idea of the meaning of "charismatic"; what they acknowledged was that things were pulled off when Stepan Razin was in command, even though he was not one of the "naked," as his family had long left the Voronezh area. His father, Timofey must have been among the "house owners." He had gotten one of the most influential figures and would be hetman of the Don host to stand as godfather to his son born some time around 1630. Compared to Timofey, the mother was of rather low origins: a Turkish woman whose name we do not know, part of the booty Timofey had taken in some raid. As his mother died young, Stenka was raised by a certain Matriona Govoruha, a talkative woman if the evidence of her name is to be believed. The first source to mention Stepan Razin is dated 1652, the year when the boy petitioned the assembly at Cherkassk, the Don host's capital, to be allowed to keep the promise he had made his dying father to visit the miraculous saints at the Solovetsky monastery. We also know about some other journeys he made in those years when, as a member of Cossack delegations, he went to Moscow and Astrakhan. Here the Cossacks must have made use of his wide knowledge of languages (according to a secretary of the Swedish embassy, he spoke eight) during their negotiations with the Kalmyks. These assignments show that Razin had gained some respect among the Cossacks by the 1660s. Then, in 1665, his family suffered a blow that must have had a decisive effect on Razin's later career and political temper: his brother Ivan Razin was executed by Prince Yuri Dolgoruky. What happened was that Ivan, leading Cossack troops in the current campaign of the Polish war, asked permission to be allowed to take his force back to the Don as autumn had already set in. The Cossacks went home in spite of being forbidden to leave. Later Stepan himself admitted that this case had created in him a terrible thirst for revenge.[8]

What is to be seen here again is a recurring feature of peasant rebellions: a member of the privileged class takes command of the movement. His knowledge in the arts of leading armies, familiarity with locations, commandership and grasp of social and political affairs is so superior that it elevates him way over the people he commands. It was obviously due to Razin's ability as a leader that the next plunder raid undertaken by the Upper Don Cossacks in 1667 started with far more thorough preparation than the previous ones. The "naked ones" assembled around Perevolok where the Don is closest to the Volga. They sent messages calling their fellows to follow them to the Volga and the Caspian, and the number of fighting men began to approach the thousand mark. The food and equipment necessary for the campaign were either ransomed from the rich Cossacks or bought from them at interest. In May 1667 they felt ready to move and marched towards the Volga.

The reason for and purposes of their action were prosaic though understandable, but not by the Voevoda Andrei Unkovsky of Tsaritsyn to whom Razin explained: "The host has nothing to eat or drink, the sovereign's donations of money and grains are getting low so the Cossacks will go to the Volga to feed themselves...."[9] In the spirit of the declaration the Cossacks looted ships sailing down the river and had no sense of committing sacrilege when plundering a ship of the patriarch's or the tsar's. Yet the very fact that the fifteen hundred Cossacks in thirty-five boats passed the large fortresses along the river and reached the mouth of the Volga borders on the miraculous. The garrison of every fortress engaged them or fired on them, usually with the intention of driving these militant Cossacks away from their towns. Finally the raiders arrived at the fortress of Yaitsky. Here Razin and forty comrades got into the fortress dressed as pilgrims and opened the gates for their comrades in hiding outside. The defenders either changed sides or were killed by the Cossacks.

This was something Moscow could not ignore. It became more or less clear in the center that they were now dealing with something different from the usual Cossack raid. In addition to the material loss, the tsar's authority was suffering terrible moral damage at the hands of the Cossacks, who were creating an antagonistic mood by setting slaves free and by wooing tsarist soldiers over to them. But Razin did not want a battle with the tsar's army that was approaching them. Having spent the winter at Yaitsky, he set sail on the high seas. The real adventure was only to begin now.

The Cossack fleet of forty vessels and two thousand men now shaped itself into a proper buccaneering enterprise. They were hunting for rich merchantmen in Persian waters and ravaged the coastline between Derbent and Baku several times. True, at the very beginning, they had sent envoys to the shah to inquire whether he might need their services; they had, however, continued looting all the same. The Persians' answer came without delay: two envoys were torn apart by dogs, and the others were circumcised. Nevertheless the delay served the Cossacks: sometimes by ruse, sometimes by force, they looted a score of thriving settlements, often with shocking violence. Contemporary foreign observers say that in Astrabad, after feasting with the local khan, the Cossacks massacred the male population and abducted eight hundred women. Then, after an orgy that lasted three weeks, they threw the women into the sea to pacify the wrathful sea god.[10]

When winter had set in, the army drew back to the Mian Kaleh Peninsula between Astrabad and Farahabad. The Cossacks' position was worsening with the passing of time. The Persians did not cease to attack them, and the following spring, while continuing the raids, they encountered fierce resistance offered by the Turkomans. The size of the Cossack force constantly shrank as a result. Finally the Persian fleet arrived, and the decisive naval encounter took place in June. Through a masterly ruse, the Cossacks scattered an enemy superior in numbers. They pretended to have lost control of their ships, running heedlessly. Seeing that, the Persians chained their ships together and tried to herd the Cossacks toward the shore. At that point the Cossacks turned their guns on the Persian flagship and capsized it. The sinking vessel began to pull the other vessels down with it as well. Before they sank, the Cossacks grappled with the enemy and in the ensuing combat mercilessly slaughtered the Persians. However, their victory was Pyrrhic since their losses, too, were huge and an even larger Persian fleet soon put out against them; all they could do was return home.

But the forts along the Volga were still there and no longer as unsuspecting as when the Cossack ships on their downward journey had slipped through. Rather than fighting the alerted forts, the

Cossack leader favored negotiation, which the tsar's government also supported. Thus on August 22, 1669, the decimated army was able to march ceremoniously into the town of Astrakhan to the sound of cheering residents and the garrison's cannon salute. Stepan Razin, grand-master of ambush and Cossack attack, now appeared to be the soberly calculating tactician that the situation demanded, successfully protecting his people (and booty). Willing to sacrifice money to his purposes, he bribed all the local officials including the voevoda himself.

He even thought of getting his soldiers to display some of their fabulous oriental treasures, sell some at bargain prices in the local bazaar and scatter coins to the poor. It is easy to understand why Razin's popularity skyrocketed overnight. Simple folk now regarded him as a hero, out of their own fables, and addressed him as "batko"—dear father.

This enterprising band of Cossacks reveled in their glory for two weeks before they could be persuaded to move out of the town. Although Razin had to hand over the heavy guns and his mace, the symbol of his authority, he could still leave with his head held high. The Cossacks sailed on in arms and with their booty (including horses that the shah of Persia had sent to the tsar) and their captives. They even managed to prevent the drawing up of a list of the names of those who had taken part in the raid. From this point their home-coming was legitimate as they had had no hesitation to send a dele-gation to tearfully apologize to Tsar Alexis Mikhailovich. Exploiting the situation he was in, Razin could afford to pull the beard of the voevoda in Tsaritsyn and to let all the prisoners free.[11]

The Cossacks arrived back to the Don and did not disperse. Instead, Razin had a fortress erected on the island between the vil-lages of Kagalnitsky and Vedernikovsky and settled there. He then plunged into organizing his army without regard to cost, and by next spring he had a force of four to five thousand armed men, training them in murderously severe military exercises. In these months there was to all practical purposes two centers of power for the Don host. The "house owning" dignitaries were at Cherkassk, while at a distance of two days' travel were Stenka's forces, blockading Cherkassk. No one had any idea what these large preparations were for. That was made clear in March 1670. Accompanied by his men, Razin appeared at the great Cossack assembly at Cherkassk and asked the leading Cossacks gathered there which direction they wanted to start fighting in. Towards Azov? The Cossacks were silent. Against the boyars in Russia? Few said yes. "Shall we go perhaps to the Volga?" was his last question, and the Cossacks broke out shouting in joy.[12]

"The naked ones" had thus chosen the familiar path. In fact, another possibility was broached but was not unanimously backed. The tsar's administrators were not happy about the Volga route either. They had good reason to be concerned, since Razin revealed the Cossacks' destination by saying: "We are going to the Volga to meet the boyars." In the appropriate spirit they then drowned some of the "spies" sent from Moscow and beat the rest to death in front of the terrorized and speechless "house owners." The social aspect of the deeds the "naked" Cossacks now come to be expressed as their purpose, which went beyond simple looting. They would launch their new campaign not only for plunder but also to teach a lesson to the wicked boyars. Their offensive, however, would be directed against the sovereign's "bad advisers." Respect for the tsar was not diminished in the Cossacks' eyes; they regarded the tsar himself as being far above these everyday concerns.

In early May 1670 Razin moved his force in the direction of Perevolok. During an assembly held in the middle of the month at the village of Panshin he gave their accumulated rage an ideological frame: "Would you desire to march on the Volga from the Don and then turn against Russia from the Volga to drive the boyar traitors and the Duma people out of the state of Moscow and the voevodas and prikaz clerks out of the town?"[13] The raiding party had become a Cossack revolt, a fact that the leader made quite clear by announcing the liberation of the "black" men, the serfs.

But much of the Cossacks' intention is revealed by the fact that they differentiated between "good" and "wicked" boyars. They were not aiming at toppling the whole system, least of all at removing the tsar, which Razin found necessary to emphasize theatrically by unsheathing his sword and shouting that, should he ever raise a hand against the sovereign, let his own weapon separate his head from his trunk. Thus the movement was launched, for the benefit of the tsar, to defend him against malevolent advice. This is why the almost simultaneous and unexpected deaths of the tsarina and the two tsareviches, Alexis and Simeon, received such heavy stress among the arguments voiced at the gathering. The Cossacks attributed those deaths to the boyars.

In its aims and ideology therefore this revolt was similar to other agrarian rebellions. This time, however, a crack army of seasoned fighting men were involved, led by an exceptional individual. Stepan Razin had proved his talent, determination and cunning several times over, getting his men out of tight corners by means of ruses. These were then widely spoken of, colored and modified, finally enveloping the *batiushka* in the mystical haze of legend. The miracles in fact often had rather straightforward explanations. For instance, when the Cossacks had first sailed past Tsaritsyn, the gunners of the fortress, sympathizing with them, fired blanks at the Cossacks, who were absolutely convinced that they were witnessing a miracle; thanks to their leader, no bullet could wound them. Thus was born a charismatic leader whose command could push them beyond the bounds of a looting party.

By the time Razin arrived at Tsaritsyn, his first destination, his army had swelled to seven thousand. The city's people opened the gates before him, the hated officials were executed, rich burghers' homes were looted and an assembly was called. The same sequence would be repeated several times in a bone-chilling choreography along the rebels' route, which now led away from Moscow, towards the southern town of Astrakhan. The Cossacks turned south perhaps to protect their backs, perhaps to widen their support and certainly because the core of Razin's force had very pleasant memories of that town. Before their arrival there, they defeated yet another tsarist army and this time without bloodshed; the tsar's soldiers ran up to the Cossacks, hugged and kissed them and declared that they too wanted to fight the boyar traitors. Almost the identical scene was played out in Astrakhan, a town normally impossible to take by siege. The defenders were crushed by the pressure exerted by city people from within and Cossacks from without. Razin spent a month in the town and, after the looting and drinking bouts usual on such occasions, introduced strict military order—based on the Cossack principle of equality. Slaves and serfs were set free and every document referring to the superior-subordinate relationship was destroyed. With that finished, the Cossacks set out north again along the Volga on July 20, 1670.

Back at Tsaritsyn, they again discussed the direction they should continue in. The fact that now they had three choices (the Don, the steppe and along, the Volga to Moscow) reveals their irresolution. Finally they voted for the original decision, the Volga, but they also made attempts to induce other areas to rise as well. An army went to the Don and the northern Donets. Another was needed to neutralize the "house-owning" Cossacks who had remained behind. The number of men in the main army, however, did not suffer for the departure of so many seasoned soldiers, as its ranks swelled consistently as they advanced on the Volga, especially along the middle section of the river where Razin's incendiary manifestoes and the news of his army's victorious march drew great masses of peasants to him.[14] Thus the Cossack revolt was slowly growing into a peasant war in which the seeds of the movement's eventual destruction were being harbored. The army was being diluted by the peasants, its military prowess was declining and its supply of arms was growing inadequate. The single-mindedness and unity of the Cossack venture were no longer there. This heterogenous mass could not be held together by a single Cossack leader however capable Razin was.

From late summer 1670 on, the peasants, boatmen and vagabonds crowding to see the Cossack fleet sailing up the Middle Volga saw a peculiar boat. It was covered in red velvet, and no one was allowed to approach it. Truly a phantom boat, its oars also plunged into the water when the army started to move and it proceeded with the other vessels; yet, no one ever saw its passenger. The crowd's curiosity was satisfied, for the Cossacks readily "disclosed" that the Tsarevich Alexis was on board under guard, defended from the boyars' murderous plots, to be taken back in safety to Moscow where he belonged.

Even if we refrain from taking the Cossacks at their word (they were never short of a few white lies), we are still facing an unexpected inconsistency. Hardly a few months before, these very same Cossacks had grieved over the death of the tsarevich, praying for his soul, turning against the boyar traitors to take vengeance for him. Now they were claiming that the tsarevich was trusting himself to their care. We can thus suspect that this false tsar tale was invented not for the Cossacks but for the large but mixed throng that was joining them in order to legitimize the "God-incited" peasant war. That was not enough for the Cossacks. Since they had to meet the wishes of the widest possible popular support, they held a further mystery in reserve by taking another phantom boat along. This one was wrapped in black velvet for the sake of variety and was supposed to be carrying the exiled Patriarch Nikon. As the former church leader was (unlike the tserevich) still alive, this story had at least a trace of reality. What is more, Razin's people had actually tried to contact Nikon, but he had rebuffed them. We cannot tell who was sitting in that mysterious boat. Most likely, no one. But as to the boat in red velvet, that might have carried a person. It was, of course, not Alexis but a former prisoner, the Tartar Prince Andrei Cherkassky who, naturally, preferred not to show his face to the crowd. Here, therefore, we have a rudimentary version of the false-tsar belief which, in effect, was serving as an ideological last resort. The restrained use of the myth can be explained, of course, by something more than its mere auxiliary function. More likely, no appropriate substitute had been found this time and, an even more important consideration, Razin did not want to relinquish command, as Bolotnikov had done, to a "Tsarevich Peter." Yet the effectiveness of even such a distorted form of the false-tsar tale was demonstrated by Razin's Cossack fighters; they would fall upon the enemy with their terrible battle cry of "Nitchay!" (for unfathomable reasons this is what they called the invisible tsarevich) to indulge in yet another massacre.[15]

Astrakhan was followed by Saratov and Samara. The inhabitants opened the gates there too, receiving the rebels with bread and salt. The next town, Simbirsk proved to be a tougher (as it turned out later, uncrackable) nut for Razin's army. Though they succeeded in taking the town, the fortress resisted them for a full month. Meanwhile, the uprising had spread over vast territories. War was raging all along the Volga as well as north of it, on the Don, in the Nizhegorod district and elsewhere. But the contacts maintained between the rebel centers were loose, and their resistance lacked coordination. Furthermore the passage of time favored the court, which sent a large army under Prince Yuri Dolgoruky to Simbirsk. There was never any doubt about the final outcome of the decisive battle against a regular army of considerable force. Razin himself was gravely wounded; he was taken from the field by a handful of his men, who got him a boat and escaped north towards the Don. Here we can see the tragic mistake Razin had made by failing to put his house in order. In the spring, the rich "house-owning" Cossacks of his home settlement arrested him, and it was none other than his godfather, the Hatman Kornilo Yakovlev, who handed him over to the tsar's men. His fate was sealed. He accepted death with the calm that befits great men. The lyrical and simple words he spoke to console and encourage Frol, his younger brother of lesser endurance, still survive: "...remember how much you had out of life, how long you lived among friends in honor and glory, remember the thousands upon thousands of men you could command, and so accept your hard fate now with tolerance...."[16] He preserved his dignity as a man to the last moment. Before a silent crowd in Red Square, when the executioner first cut off his right hand and then his left foot before beheading him, "... he revealed no weakness of soul not even with a sign," an eyewitness wrote.

The leader was dead but the uprising was not over yet. Isolated pockets of resistance continued for a long time until they were all mercilessly reduced: in a single town, Arzamas. Eleven thousand rebels were hanged or beheaded. Thus Stepan Razin's goal remained unfulfilled. In his words, he had come to bring liberty. This did not come about because he himself had not been quite sure of his intentions. Wherever he had set himself, he had organized the environment upon the Cossack pattern. But what would have happened if he had managed to take Moscow? Would he have tried to establish a Cossack republic? That is unlikely, since even he had remained part of the system when launching his campaign to save the tsar and to persecute only the "evil" boyars. However, after the introduction of the false Alexis, this idea too was modified to an extent. Great numbers swore fealty in the "invisible" tsarevich's name (rather than in that of the tsar on the throne) and were promised that the "tsarevich" would show them his face after Novgorod was successfully besieged. Thus Razin must have prepared for the possibility of Tsar Alexis Mikhailovich's being reluctant to "agree" with him. Like so many of his naive contemporaries, he expected too much of the tsar. He is recorded to have believed in having managed to "open the tsar's eyes," even while in the open cart that took him in chains to Moscow.[17]

If we can say that the resistance survived the death of its leader, it is a thousand times truer for the Razin legend. His heroic deeds were being sung even in his lifetime; his memory was saved by folk songs. His prestige pushed even the false-tsar legend into the shadows. Peculiarly, however, that legend did not die either after the rebels' defeat even though the authorities were experienced in battling against such beliefs. Tsarist ordinances from the autumn of 1670 reported the exact circumstances of the tsarevich's death, and in order to achieve the fullest credit, two or three people from every district were summoned to Moscow to see the truth for themselves. Despite all this, a false Alexis appeared again in the township of Toropets in the autumn of 1671, after Razin's execution. This one did show his face to the people, though he may have fared better if he had not done so. It soon turned out that Ivan Kleopin, a lunatic, was the man who disturbed the authorities, which, in turn, showed no mercy when it came to dealing with false tsars. Though it became clear during torture that they had a madman on their hands (orthodoxy had always regarded madness as akin to holiness), Ivashka Kleopin was speedily hanged.[18]

Moscow had far more trouble two years later with a new false tsarevich who chose the name of Simeon, the other dead son of the tsar. Hetman Samoylovich of the Eastern Ukraine, which was under Russian domination, reported that the Zaporozhe Cossacks were showing great respect to a young man of uncertain age and long, tanned face whose body was said to be adorned with the stigma of tsars (crown, bent sword, double-headed eagle, moon and stars). Later these turned out to be simple spots that ruined his complexion. Since the Cossacks did not hand over the "thief," the authorities sent its "specialists" to Zaporozhe speedily with orders to seize the false tsarevich.

Scenes ensued at Zaporozhe. In a drunken fit of boasting the false Simeon roundly cursed the Russians and one of them shot at him. This caused the Cossacks to lock up the Russian emmissaries under heavy guard and Serko, the Cossacks' hetman, sent a complaint to the tsar. In his letter he claimed that the false tsarevich was genuine and retold the adventurer's tale, according to which the false tsar had been insulted by his "uncle," the boyar Miloslavsky, and wounded by his mother who had even wanted to have him killed. So he had fled to Razin's camp and came on to the Ukrainian Cossacks from the Don. The hetman's words make it clear why the local Cossacks had been trusting. The tsar's subsidies were too little and the Cossacks were gravely insulted because somebody else had been appointed over their Hetman Serko chief hetman of the Eastern Ukraine. In fact, Semion came to them as a blessing; well aware of the tsarist administration's fear of the false-tsar legends, they wanted to blackmail the government through the new impostor.

The Zaporozhe Cossacks' reasoning was not unrealistic. At that time there was considerable rivalry between the Cossacks of Hetman Samoylovich living on the Don's left bank and those of Hetman Petr Doroshenko on the right bank. The rivalry between them was, of course, more than a clash of private interests; the questions of Cossack autonomy and orientation towards the neighboring peoples and states were also raised. It was thus not at all indifferent to Moscow whether the Zaporozhe Cossacks, belonging to neither faction, would stand with Doroshenko in leaning towards Crimean and Turkish help or would stand with the Russian-oriented Samoylovich. Serko's people cleverly exploited the delicate balance. Their trump card was the false tsarevich. But Samoylovich soon overcame his opponent with Russian aid, and on March 17, 1674, the merger of the two Ukraines under his leadership was announced in Pereyaslavl. Serko then took a complete turn, and in demonstration of his loyalty, he sent the false Simeon to Moscow. His reward came as due: his Cossacks received their grain, felt, lead and gunpowder; Serko himself received sables worth 114 rubles.[19]

In a Moscow torture chamber everything came to light of course. Simeon was a Pole from the vicinity of Warsaw. He had been sold several times before managing to escape to the Cossacks. On the Don he had met Hetman Miyussky who led the remnants fighting on after Razin's death; with this struggle becoming more and hopeless, Miyussky led a few men to the cataracts of the Dnieper looking for support. There he met Semion Vorobyov just in time to appoint him tsarevich and thus gain supportive means of the false-tsarevich ploy. The hetman was trying to revive his movement in the traditional way. The balance of political power, however, worked against him in the Ukraine as well. His creature, the child who had assumed the impostor's role with surprising speed, shared the great Razin's fate. In a sense he was honored by being carried to Moscow on the same cart and executed in exactly the same way as the "batko."[20] "Tsarevich Simeon," alias Simeon Vorobyov, was a ripple following the giant wave of the Cossack and peasant war. But this unimportant individual's undeservedly spectacular execution demonstrated fear the system had of popular resistance and the false-tsar legends that could mobilize it.

Chapter 6

THE ANTICHRIST TSAR
AND HIS FALSE SONS

The idea of opening windows to the West occurred to rulers of Russia long before Peter I's time. Boris Godunov was the first tsar to send young men to the West to study. His efforts, however, came to naught because the students never returned to their native land. The military defeats suffered during the Time of Troubles made Moscow realize that traditional military equipment and tactics were no longer adequate to wage war against their western neighbors. Importing Western troops and arms became an urgent necessity. This was the beginning of the penetration of Western ideas and customs into Russian life, though both the official and the schismatic churches of Russia did their utmost to obstruct the process. Since the army and the government needed the presence of the West, the churches were unable to effectively resist it and were forced to retire with their militant philippics to the battlefield of ideology. There, of course, those who advocated "Latin," "Greek," and "German" orientation (not to mention those of the Old Belief who labeled the other three as heretical) fell upon each other with virulent hatred; nevertheless, by the time Peter came to the throne, the West had irrevocably entered Russian life—suffice it to mention the widespread fashion of trimming beards, wearing "German" clothing, furnishing homes with mirrors, carved chairs and tables and, in the homes of the nobility, cheap engravings.[1]

To date exactly Peter's inauguration is not easy. Although, after slightly over five years of his brother Fedor's reign, Peter was declared tsar in 1682; the coup his half-sister Sophia organized immediately snatched power from him and appeared to bestow it on his mentally ill brother Ivan. Peculiarly, Peter remained co-tsar, though as "number two" only. Actual power was in the hands of the regent Sophia whom Peter was only able to topple two years later. Even then, he had to wait another seven years to become sole monarch upon Ivan's death. Meanwhile, of course, the child Peter had grown into adolescence and adulthood; the adult Peter decided it was time to play real soldiers, after exercising his toy battalions long enough. However, the catastrophic attempt to retake the fortress of Azov from the Turks showed him that a naval war was impossible without ships. Since modern ships were made in the West, the tsar set off abroad to study shipbuilding and, once in the West, to patch an alliance of some kind against the Turks.

We have had ample opportunity to read of Peter I's Western journey, the "grand embassy," which was quite unprecedented in Russian history, as no crowned ruler of Russia had ever gone abroad voluntarily.[2] What interests us now is not the events of the journey, which could be featured in comedies and and fairy tales, but the fact that Peter's reforms began right then. Arriving home with maximum speed to the news of the streltsy revolt of 1698, the tsar set an example of terrible cruelty. Only then did he announce that the wearing of long beards and flowing robes was prohibited. To lay emphasis on his decree, he himself cut off the beards of some boyars. Naturally, he did not ignore the treasury's needs, so the new laws had an important loophole: the lower estates were allowed to retain their hairy looks after paying a beard tax and could prove their privilege by producing a huge stamp on demand. That, by the way, was the first augury of a policy of collecting taxes on the basis of astonishing excuses. The money was needed this time for the Great Northern War, started in order to gain an outlet to the Baltic ports. Since Peter's long reign featured only one single year in which war was not consuming the country's resources, we can imagine the burden on the population. The newly introduced head tax alone trebled the sum that peasants had had to pay. The draft, forcing those young men unfortunate to be chosen into lifelong military service, was also heavy a blow. The glorious conquests might justify measures that exploited the largest numbers of the Russian people to an extent never known before. Yet, seen from the aspect of our theme, it is far more important to examine how the people reacted to a new and incomparably more difficult situation.

This was time for false tsars, we might think, since these had always had greatest success during periods of crises, when the people experienced extraordinary hardship. Until now we saw that the popular anger leading to open revolt was always brought to the surface by the false tsar belief.[3] However, this time, although the social tensions threatening to explode were present and paved the way for a major uprising on the part of peasants and Cossacks under the command of Hetman Kondrati Bulavin, there was no trace of the false-tsar belief. This proves a number of things, including the point that the emergence of false tsars and the shaping of a false-tsar legend is not at all so automatic and mechanical a process has to be a necessary consequence of grave social problems. Bulavin's crushed revolt also saves us from the hasty conclusion that only the false-tsar belief was able to mobilize peasant resistance in Russia. In a particular sense the false-tsar legend has a life of its own, which might (as it usually did) coincide with social problems; but in order to function, it also needs the presence of a host of other conditions. For instance, the tsar must die under—possibly—suspicious circumstances so his idolized memory can be awakened. He must be popular (or, at least die before disappointing the religious faith in him) and whoever impersonates him would do very well to look like him, especially in the case of such an unmistakably original character as Tsar Peter was.

Lacking these conditions, no false tsar can emerge. That, however, does not hinder the masses of people from looking on the lawful tsar on the throne with a hatred that is hardly in harmony with their traditional respect for the tsar; yet the false-tsar legend operates here as well. Obviously they cannot point at a "real" tsar, but they are absolutely convinced that the ruler in the Kremlin must be a false tsar. Even the blind can see that: how else would it be possible for a tsar "ruling by the grace of God" to perform such acts of sacrilege as throwing out our fathers' customs, cutting off beards, dressing up his subjects in heretical clothes, adding to his flock's many problems with choice torments? This is why, beginning with Peter's first decree and increasing through the years, a growing part of the population firmly believed that this monster must be none other than the Antichrist himself.

The following Orthodox legend was in circulation even in the nineteenth century:

> Once, as the tsar was just preparing to demolish the Old Belief forever, he walked among the tall trees in the woods along the Neva bank, lost in thought. "My people do not love me," he muttered to himself, "they call me the Antichrist and turn away from me." As he was thus tormenting himself, he did not notice he had lost his way. In his trouble now he crossed himself in his ancestors' way and an old holy man immediately appeared before him and said these words: "You are the Antichrist, blinded by Satan. Everlasting darkness will cover you until you make your sins good." The old man disappeared and Peter fell into a deep sleep. In his dream, he grew a beard and donned full-length clothes and then, when he woke up, a voice from heaven spoke to him. He said "Cross yourself three times

and sit on your throne. But the tsar, however he tried, was unable to sit on the throne which kept moving farther and farther away from him. Peter blindly followed the throne. After a long and tormenting journey his strength waned. Finally he collapsed on the ground and wheezed, "Lord, take my soul unto Thyself..." and then rigor mortis set in. Now God-fearing Old Believers came out of the woods and buried the tsar according to the ancient rituals.

His body was dead but his soul was flying free. Disturbing thoughts tormented him: "I wonder who is leading my country now? It must be Lefort and the boyars, who defile the true faith and will put my son Alexis to death." And indeed, after hearing that the tsar had disappeared, the boyars gathered. They decided they could not manage without a ruler. But for the moment they decided on telling the people that the tsar had gone abroad and was residing there, then they quickly got a man, one who was the tsar's identical image, to avoid the people finding out the truth. Lefort and the boyar Streshniev came together and chose a relative of the latter to be the tsar. That man was really Peter's perfect look-alike.

Since then, Russia had two tsars: a real one doing penance in his grave for his sins, and a false one sitting on the throne and committing all kinds of hideous crimes against his Orthodox subjects. He burned a multitude of people alive in their houses,

had even more beheaded or drowned. The
pain that enveloped the people cannot be
told or described: like a river, the pain flooded Russia.[4]

The legend goes on at a leisurely pace. It recalls even an encounter
between the re-converted real tsar and the false one, featuring a
number of miracles but ending with the false tsar burning the real
one. Yet, the latter's bones are not found, and the martyred tsar
flies away in the form of a dove. The crowned tsar starts thinking
hard over these facts, and from that time on, the Old Believers are
not sent to die in fire.

All the necessary ingredients of religious tales are here: the
falling into sin and cleansing, mercy and cruelty, good battling
evil, even a sorrowful kind of happy ending. But it is still more
important to realize that the legend faithfully reflects the popular
mood and tempers, listing also the exact historical grievances.
This time, in response to the special situation prevailing in Peter's
day, the traditional pattern of "good tsar—wicked boyars" included also "mean foreign counselors." Another important feature of
the legend is that the tsar himself is divided into two personalities,
a "real" and a "false" one. The twist in the story that conjoins the
sovereign's replacement with Peter's western journey is also characteristic and instructive.

This legend was born among the schismatics; thus, understandably, it approaches the tsar's character from a point of religious grievance. Since the peasants in Russia were hardly affected by Nikon's church reforms and remained Old Believers almost
to the last, their only form of protest was clearly the defense of
their religion. It is not an accident that social grievances also
appear in the legend. In this respect we are offered invaluable evidence by the files of the bureau responsible for state security, the
so-called Preobrazhensky Prikaz (Board).

The Preobrazhensky Board was quite literally a devilish institution. Its most important task was to uncover "plots" against the sovereign and the state. Although plotting was mostly in abeyance for the duration of Peter's absolutism, no despotic reign could ever take enough precautions against them. Thus it was enough to utter a careless remark, say, about the new clothes over a few drinks, and the customer was dragged out of the tavern and into the bureau's torture chambers right away. There were always volunteers who regarded it as their duty to report a "case." Most often, naturally, the way of winding up such "cases" was as follows: on being arrested, common criminals often tried to avoid summary execution or exile by claiming that they had some information on certain affairs concerning opposition to the tsar. The process against them was immediately put aside, and a new investigation was launched into the new case. As it took long months to complete inquiries, the original criminal sometimes got away with a reward instead of punishment.

This was what happened to a certain Dorofey Veselkov who was arrested in 1723 for minting counterfeit money in Tobolsk and brought to Moscow immediately. Here he announced he wanted to uncover traitors. The essence of his report was that in the previous year he had been at the village of Mezshevaya Utka where certain peasants had said that the tsar was ruining the chapels and icons. What is more, a nun called Platonida had added that the ruler was in fact an "exchanged" Swede, which is why he crossed himself in the Swedish way, wore Swedish clothes and had married a Swedish woman. Moreover, he had locked his wife up in a nunnery and exterminated his son Alexis; his grandson, born by a Swedish woman, had come to the world with a tooth in his mouth; in all, the tsar was the Antichrist himself. In the ensuing investigation all the peasants of the faraway Siberian village concerned were tracked down, brought to the capital and interrogated. Two nuns (one of them aged 70) died during the inquisition, and a third died on the way to Moscow. Veselkov, the counterfeiter was set free and received a reward.[5]

The archives of the Preobrazhensky Board preserve reports on a large number of similar cases. Of course, not all informers fared so well; in most cases they also became tainted as those denounced returned the favor. From these cases we can conclude that the identification of Peter with the Antichrist was widespread. It was often coupled with apocalyptic visions of the approaching end of the world. In one of these, the tsar will occupy Rome and Constantinople, then he will assemble the Jews and march against Jerusalem. There he will grow fond of the Jews and start to reign over them, a terrible time of poverty will come. The Jews will also recognize the tsar as the Antichrist and the end of the world will arrive.

Peter even provided "proof" of his "being a devil" for the simple folk: he had the newly press-ganged soldiers' hands branded as a precaution against mass desertion. Simple people were inclined to regard those brands as the devils handiwork.

Nevertheless, we also know of contemporary rumors in which the belief that Peter was an exchanged false tsar is not directly linked with the Antichrist tale. "What kind of a tsar is that man?" exclaimed a peasant in the torture chamber. "He is a thief, a breaker of oaths, he was exchanged for a German! He gave the tsar's power to the boyars and converted to the pagan faith and went with the Germans to where the wind blew him. On fasting days, Wednesday and Friday, he eats meat. It is time he were impaled on the stake...." It was a widespread belief among the people that Peter was not Russian but German. Some thought he was born in Moscow's "German" settlement; others supposed his mother, Natalya Kirillovna had exchanged her infant daughter for a German baby boy out of fear of her husband. Another common belief was that the tsar was the son of his own confidant, the "alien" François Lefort.[6]

A series of stories upon the following pattern is known:

> The sovereign and his men were abroad,
> visiting the German lands, and the tsar

> spent some time in Stekol (Stockholm).
> The Stekoli country (Sweden) is ruled by a
> female, and that female cursed the sover-
> eign and made him sit in a hot pan, then
> took him off it and jailed him.

According to this version, Peter escaped, thanks to a self-sac-
rificing *strelets* (musketeer). Other versions feature another ending in which the tsar is bundled into a barrel and pushed into the
sea. In the years following the "grand embassy" journey, the basic
idea was richly ornamented: gossip had the tsar killed in several
countries, exchanged with a number of subjects of different
nationalities and faced with widely diverse fates in remote foreign
lands. All versions agreed on one point, that the "real" tsar was
either dead or in trouble abroad, while the one in the Kremlin had
taken his place by fraud.[7]

Strangely enough, Peter himself did his best to nourish such
gossip. Simple folk in the street had to see that something was
wrong about the tsar. On the occasion of a triumphal march into
Moscow following the victory at Azov, the troops were led by
General Sein and Admiral Lefort and the tsar came on foot behind
the admiral's gold-studded sleigh, bearing the name of Captain
Petr Alexeyev. Actually, he often called himself just "Peter" or—
during his Western tour—Petr Mikhailov. His travelling incogni-
to was not necessary for any "political" consideration even in this
instance, as everybody knew who the humbler versions of Peter's
name were referring to. The real cause for his eccentric behavior
is far more likely to have been his intention to express contempt
for traditional hierarchy. Indeed, he was quite fond of anti-estab-
lishment mannerisms and bizarre eccentricities which, especially
in the first years of his reign, were often elevated into government
policy. One of his most astounding acts was founding the college
for heavy drinking, "The All-Joking, All-Drunken Synod of Fools
and Jesters" headed by a "Prince-Pope."

The great Russian historian Vasily Klyuchevsky (1841–1911) wrote that Peter himself made up its statutes, demonstrating no less legislative talent than in any other of his decrees. Peter credited here a parody of the church hierarchy with its costumes, prayer books, sinners and even foolish priestesses and abbesses. They even had a drinking ritual titled "On serving Bacchus and treating spirits honestly." When inaugurating a new member, they asked: "Do you drink?" in parody of the church's "Do you believe?" Often the "pious assembly," having performed the sacrifice to Bacchus, scrambled onto sledges and, amid shouts and whistles, drove into town to paint it red. Dressed as a patriarch, the Prince-Pope Nikita Zotov, Peter's old tutor, was in the lead. He deserved this honor by always being the the drunkest member of the company. Characteristically Peter held only the title of "protodeacon" even in this company.[8]

Thus the tsar discarded tradition spectacularly, desecrating even the visual display of his "God-given" power, which alone "proved" a sovereign's "genuineness" to his simple Orthodox subjects. He himself made it absolutely clear for everybody that he was a "false" tsar. Yet the redeemer, the "real" tsar was not coming, though everything was done to bring him on the scene. But there was not a man even remotely resembling Peter's looks, and the despotic regime was too strong for a simple impostor to try his wiles on. This is true even though we know that some false tsars did emerge in Peter's time. For it was not his name they assumed but that of his son Alexis.

The example of these false tsareviches shows that the false-tsar belief flourishes especially in those situations in which the tsar or a member of his family dies unexpectedly in suspicious circumstances and in a way incomprehensible to the people. It is exactly these high persons' "divinity" that makes their passing incredible and gives the people a hope of their posthumous escape. And as regards Alexis Petrovich, he actually did die in hair-raising and hardly comprehensible circumstances.

To be able to interpret the events on the day of his death, we must marginally touch upon the conflict between father and son that went far beyond the usual distance between two generations, being more of the dimension of Greek tragedy. As far as it can be judged today, Alexis was his father's opposite in every respect, except for his mental abilities. While the father exploited his talents mostly in the field of practical action, the tsarevich was more of a passive type, which was something his father could never accept. For a time Peter insisted on reforming his son, like his country, by force, but in the end he gave up the hopeless effort. Though Alexis submitted himself to his father's will, he did so reluctantly, leaving no doubt about how much against his better judgement he was acting. Peter was a source of constant physical and mental torment to his son. Charecteristically, when his father wanted to test his skill at draughtsmanship, the tsarevich preferred putting a bullet through his hand out of his fear of failing the examination. (Incidentally, he could not even shot himself through the hand properly.)[9]

It was also under pressure from his father that the tsarevich chose a wife; then, when the tsar's grandson was born, Peter, ever tactful, now a grandfather, sent a letter to his son on the day of the young mother's death. In the letter he threatened to exclude his son from his inheritance, should the tsarevich fail to change his attitude. Alexis hastened to answer that he would renounce his claim to the throne with pleasure. He signed his reply "the humblest servant and son, Alexis." But the tsar was still not satisfied. Less than three months later his son received another strict order: "It is impossible to remain on both sides of the fence: either change your character and desire to be an heir without hypocrisy, or go and become a monk." To hammer his point home, Peter scrawled at the bottom of the letter that if his son did not make up his mind fast, "I will treat you as I treat criminals." Understandably, the answer was not tardy in coming: "I wish to become a monk," Alexis revealed the next day.[10]

Still not satisfied with the answer, Peter refused to accept the fact that his son was unwilling to follow his example. He sent him more threatening letters, this time from his camp abroad during a campaign. Always terrified of his father, Alexis panicked when he realized that he would not have any freedom, even to retreat to a monastery, until his father died. Accordingly, taking advantage of the tsar's absence, he too went abroad, seeking refuge with his relative, the Holy Roman emperor. But he was not left alone even in far-off Naples. Peter's men caught up with him, threatening and cajoling him into returning home. The tsar guaranteed his safety both orally and in writing. After his arrival back to Moscow, everything proceeded according to the scenario. The son repented, renouncing his claim to the throne in public, and the father expressed his forgiveness, dropping all accusations against him.

Fate, however, had a different end in store for the tsarevich. An investigation began into the "plot." Without thinking, Alexis gave away the names of everybody who had known about his plan to escape. Some were executed, but the "ringleader" Alexis seemed to get off unharmed. Events soon took yet another sudden turn: as a result of Alexis's unceasing pleas, his female consort was allowed to come to Moscow. A serf's daughter, the longed-for woman brought death rather than happiness to her lover. She accused the man she loved of nothing short than desiring the tsar's death and wishing to lead the intrigue (if there had been one). This confession was confirmed by Alexis, broken by now in body and spirit, though it is hard to pinpoint today exactly what he was guilty of thinking. It should be remembered that his beautifully-composed confession to committing the capital crime was born after twenty-five lashes followed by another fifteen; it thus reflects the views of Prince Alexander Menshikov, one of the tsar's confidants assisting in the torture and interrogation, rather than those of the "offender."

Having received a free hand from the sovereign and father, the court sentenced the tsarevich to death on June 24, 1718. Two days later the tsarevich obligingly died. According to the official version prepared for foreign consumption, God came to help Peter, tormented between the conflicting sentiments of a father and a ruler, and took his son. This, of course, needed some earthly assistance as well, but that was not disclosed to the world. Some thought the tsarevich was poisoned; others supposed he was garroted.[11]

The tsar's publicly uttered and broken promise, the father's active participation in the astonishing death, made a martyr of the tsarevich, though his only political aspiration had been to stay alive. His death, however, made it possible for the people to shape him into a figure that reflected their own desire. Unable in his life to embody the anger against the tsar (though he had been well aware that the people preferred him to his father), Alexis could play this new role now that he was dead.

Tsarevich Alexis's death provided new evidence for the tsar's subjects of the "true faith" that the Antichrist was at large in Russia. But, the people reckoned, even the evil one's power is limited; the good would be rewarded sooner or later in some way. In vain did the devil try to put the good tsarevich to death; Alexis escaped and would come soon to the aid of sufferers. Alexis's legend is similar to other redeemer legends. The strength of the people's expectations concerning Alexis is shown in the fact that an army deserter named Andrei Krekshin appeared in the Nizhegorod district as early as in 1722 and made villagers believe that he was the Tsarevich Alexis. He even showed a "royal stigma" on his body as proof. He convinced the local population for three years before he was caught, lashed and sentenced to fifteen years' forced labor. Compared with earlier cases, this was a light sentence which demonstrates that his emergence had not mobilized any support. It could not have any, as Peter's system was solid enough to afford to spare the man's life.[12]

It is illusory and irresponsible to "borrow" a tsarevich's name as long as he is alive. After his death, however, the situation underwent a basic change. Much of the strength of Peter's reign is revealed by the fact that during the tsar's reign only one other false Alexis was known. This particular one came forward in the Vologda region in 1723 and turned out to be Alexei Rodionov, a poor man of Polish origin. He was mad as well, having—as neighbors stated—set his own house on fire.[13]

Immediately after the tsar's death, still in 1725, the Moscow administration received news of two false Alexises at the same time. One of them had advertised in the town of Astrakhan even in the previous year that he was the Alexis Petrovich persecuted by Menshikov. His real name was Yevstify Artiemniev; he was a soldier. In that remotest corner of the country, so very far away from the capital, he could have gone on deceiving the people forever even if had he not wished to confess his high birth in a village church. The confessor revealed without a second thought the secret of the confession in a report, and as far as Astrakhan concerned, the reign of the false tsar was cut short.[14]

St. Petersburg, however, was more concerned about the other false Alexis, who was serving in a grenadier battalion in the Ukrainian town of Pochep. He came from a solid Siberian family. His father was a sacristan. What concerned the authorities was that Tsarevich Alexei, alias Aleksandr Semikov, was circulating in a milieu that was very receptive to the false-tsar tales. Soldiers pressed into life-long service were not the most loyal servitors of the Petrine system. Moreover, the people of the Ukraine had already caused some headache to Peter by their efforts to become independent. Thus Semikov could not get off lightly. His cruel punishment had to serve as an example to all: he was beheaded and his head was put on public view along with a detailed list of his sins.[15]

The two false tsareviches of 1725 demonstrate that Peter the Great's governmental system was shaken in the wake of the death of the absolute ruler. Consequently, the following thirty-seven-year period in Russian history is known as the age of palace revolutions. It is not by chance that during this era an unusual number of false tsars appeared in Russia.

Chapter 7

EMPRESSES, MINIONS, IMPOSTORS

Frequently unwell with recurrent illness, Peter I died on January 28, 1725. His sudden death was a fitting end to his life. One day in the previous November he had been sailing down the Neva when he saw a bark in distress. None of its crew could swim, and they were waiting for death, huddling helplessly in the stormy wind. Unable to stand their misery any longer, Peter jumped into the shallow water to help. His impatient eagerness backfired: the sailors escaped and the tsar fell ill and died two months later. Although he conducted affairs with meticulous care on his deathbed, he could not arrange the succession. He was just about to write his successor's name on a piece of paper when he fell into the coma he never came out of.[1]

He delayed the decision by one minute too long, perhaps because he had already crowned his second wife as empress. This measure, in the absence of any countermanding order, legitimized rights. However, the widow's inauguration as the country's sovereign did not seen set for an easy run. Though she had spent over two decades at the court, many people still remembered Her Majesty's previous life. Katerina Skavronska, the tsar's spouse had originally been a poor Livonian girl in service with a priest at the town of Marienburg until a soldier in the Swedish army married her. In 1702, however, Marienburg fell into Russian hands, and the young woman became the personal booty of a Russian noncommissioned officer. No one would have thought that this tragic turn in her life would bring her good fortune, but this was exactly what happened. The tsar's all-powerful favorite, Menshikov noticed the perky young woman, whose charm was not lost on the tsar either. Catherine must indeed have had many allures, since Peter finally married her and had her crowned.[2]

Even those qualities would have been insufficient to have had her claim accepted without the support of Menshikov, her former lover, who led the palace guard in something close to a coup to acclaim Catherine as ruler over the Tsarevich Peter, son of the ill-fated Alexis and favorite candidate of the old aristocracy. In an ironic twist of fate two years later the boy, then eleven, would become tsar of all Russians through the assistance of the same Menshikov. During a flood, just as it happened to her husband before, Catherine was also soaked in the Neva. She had to wade in knee-high water. Chilled by the strong wind blowing from the sea, she caught a cold. Soon after, viewing a parade, she was wind chilled once more and returned to her sickbed, never to recover again. Her minion was well prepared for that eventuality and went over to the tsarevich's side. Within a few months Menshikov himself fell ill and, after recovering, was just preparing to go to the child tsar's court when he learnt that he had been exiled. Away from the capital, he soon died. In another abrupt turn, the tsar speedily followed him to the grave, dying on the very day set for his wedding.[3]

Halcyon days then began for the Moscow aristocracy. Taking advantage of Peter I's rejection of the old order of succession, they forged a new will and looked around for their most suitable candidate. The winner was the second daughter of Ivan V, Peter's former co-tsar. Anne came to Moscow from Courland after signing humiliating terms that intended to reduce the sovereign to a figurehead; supported by the palace guard, she swept those conditions aside. Her ten-year reign was a period when Baltic-German underlings (Biron, Ostermann, Münnich) ran a country in which hating officialdom now meant hating foreigners. Before dying in 1740, Anne named her sister's two-months-old grandchild as her heir, with the intention of ensuring continuing dominance of the so called "German party" in Russia. Ivan VI, however, had not even time enough to grow out of infanthood as a tsar; hardly a year after his inauguration he was toppled by Elizabeth, then thirty-one, Peter I's youngest child. The legendary hot-blooded "national" was able to have herself crowned with the considerable help of the palace guard that she was so fond of. The former tsar left his cradle and entered the prison where ha grew into childhood, adolescence and finally adulthood, when he was killed.[4]

His murder, however, took place during the reign (1762–1796) of the enlightened Catherine II (the Great) who differed from every Russian ruler before her in that she was a German with no Slav ancestors. For this reason her path to the throne was rather peculiar. From a small German ducal court she was chosen as a wife for Peter, son of Anne, Peter I's older daughter.

The nineteen years of constant humiliation while waiting for the throne made Catherine more Russian than her half-Russian husband, the heir. As soon as he gained the throne as Peter III, he immediately wanted to realize his political credo: "I would rather be a soldier in the Prussian army than a tsar of the Russians." Not surprisingly, he had no time to settle into his high office: his ambitious wife had one of her lovers strangle him in 1762.[5]

From the year 1725, four women had ruled Russia (the last occasion of a woman ruling the Russians had been almost a thousand years earlier, in Duchess Olga's time), compared to three "men," of whom one was an infant, one a boy of school age and one who even as an adult was unable to prove his manhood. These male tsars held the throne for altogether forty months, while the women rulers held it for sixty-seven years.

It was a strange century then, especially for the Orthodox subject cherishing his tsar as ruler by divine right. Just as it is difficult to imagine God or Christ as a woman, so too was it incomprehensible for the simple minds to see a woman posing as the Lord's governor on Earth. However, it was an easy enough task for a God-fearing Russian subject to cut the Gordian knot of this puzzle. The woman tsar was not a false one since each of the previously mentioned male rulers had disappeared from the Kremlin with a mysterious rapidity, so that they had no time to fulfill or disappoint the people's expectations. Since each was replaced by a woman, their fate became excellent material for false tsarship.

Catherine I, the first empress following Peter, spent too short a stint on the throne for potential false tsars to recognize their opportunity. Then, under the next tsar, Peter II, the masses had high hopes of having the old order (that before Peter I's time) restored. Their hopes were fueled by the young sovereign's moving from St. Petersburg back to the ancient capital; the prevailing mood was that of anticipation. It could be said to have been an imperative for the false tsars to appear after an absence of over half a decade when again a woman, Anne, won the throne and surrounded herself with foreign fortune hunters.

The false tsars' emergence was aided by what can be described as an accidental circumstance. In December 1731 an announcement was made concerning swearing loyalty to the heir. Unfortunately, however, there was no heir-apparent at the moment, which meant that a successor-to-be-appointed had to be ensured of his future subjects' loyalty too far in advance. This was far too sophisticated a ploy for simple minds. The man on the street could not help but be convinced that there must be an heir to the throne somewhere even though nobody actually knew where he was. Here then was a golden opportunity for self-appointed tsareviches.

They appeared in the good old way again, pretending to be Peter I's son Alexis who had all the attributes necessary for a redeemer even while he was alive. About half a dozen false tsareviches are known to have been active in the 1730s. One of them, the false Alexis of 1732 in the Tambov district, was one of the few impostors in world history who managed to have a partner in the con game.

We do not need, of course, a miracle to explain his affair. The real miracle was the fact that the barefoot monastery peasant, Timofey Truzhenik, could make others believe that it was he they had sworn loyalty to in that ominous year of 1731. In fact his success was mainly due to the soothsayer's sensing the public mood, readily recognized him as the tsarevich. This proves that there was an increasingly large number of those willing to believe in the self-appointed tsareviches at that time, indicating the worsening of social problems as well as the ripening of the conditions for heightened resistance. Well aware of the burdens of peasants near and far, Timofey promised to relieve them of the heaviest ones, such as the head tax. He did not stop there, though, and promised to bring a kind of social justice. To him this meant, as he announced, that there would be no boyars under his reign, and even if some remained, their lot would then be that of the peasants.

It would be difficult to say just how he intended to keep his promises; we suspect he did not. The words he used in an attempt to convince the initially incredulous peasants seem to reveal his true intention: "I am called Truzhenik (literally worker) because God appointed me to work," he explained to his audience. "Though I look like a muzhik, and even my hands, feet and hair resemble those of a muzhik, I am not some peasants' offspring and I will not be one. I am a tsarevich and I cannot work." The most he was willing to do was a tsarevich's share of the work.[6] In so doing, he made the peasants in the neighborhood salivate with his fantastic tales of an underground city of treasure whose wealth all be theirs sometime in return for making it possible for him to do nothing at the moment.

His stories must have had a considerable effect, since peasants made an attempt to free him when he was arrested. The most far-reaching part of his story was probably his invention of Peter, a brother tsarevich.

His "brother," originally a dragoon deserter named Larion Starodubtsev, appeared as Tsarevich Peter Petrovich. His emergence featured some of the key tricks that facilitated the mutual recognition between a leader and the mass of the people. Such an episode was his contacting the "other tsarevich." An even more important fact was that he happened to "reveal his secret" to no other than the Don Cossacks who had long been infected by the false-tsar idea. The tale he thought up was also a clever construction, featuring the story of the miraculous escape of a changeling child and the tsars' stigmata on his body. All this, however, was conjoined with some clever ideology. Larion said something like:

> The present tsar has ruined the chapels, robbed people of their jewels, forced his own religion upon us. Even I myself have suffered for my persistence in the Old Belief, sitting twice in the sovereign's prison. Now I say it is time we returned to laws of our fathers and grandfathers.

Meanwhile he had no scruples about forgetting to tell the Cossacks which tsar's son he was supposed to be. Accordingly many of the Cossacks listened suspiciously to his announcement that set the "naked" and the "house-owning" Cossacks against each other: "Let the people hear my voice," the false tsarevich Peter addressed all the downtrodden folk, "and pass it on to everybody in the market square and everywhere, let the news of me find the remotest Cossack hamlet, and then the old Cossack freedom will return!"[7]

Nevertheless, Larion Starodubtsev's loudmouthed plans were not followed by action. They could not be, for he and his "brother and colleague," Timofey Truzhenik, were caught and executed. Their followers' tongues were cut out, they were whipped and exiled to Siberia. Where Starodubtsev is concerned, we do not even know of any particular Cossack show of resistance to the false tsarevich's arrest. They apparently just looked on as their superiors surrendered their over-hasty redeemer. This false Peter may not have been a convincing leader to their taste. Or perhaps the Don Cossacks were not at that time desperate enough to believe him. Almost another forty years would pass before the usual false-tsar tale could stir considerable numbers into action. True, the tale was not put to rest in the meanwhile.

But the days of the false Alexises were soon over. The last of them made some ripples in the Ukraine in 1738. Minitsky by real name and of Polish stock, this self-appointed tsarevich talked a company of the Kiev regiment, along with the whole population of the area they were billeted in, into marching with him in regular military formation against Moscow and St. Petersburg. His venture had all the ceremonial trappings, including the oath of loyalty combined with a church service and a feu de joie. He and the priest who supported him got as far as the nearest stake; his soldiers were quartered.[8] Such was the end of Peter I's last "legitimate" false son. A few years later, in 1742, yet another son sprang out of the earth. A naval officer stationed at Tobolsk in Siberia announced that he was the great tsar's bastard son and thus loyalty should be sworn to him rather than to the half-German Karl Ulrich-Peter. An enquiry conducted by the legendary Admiral Fedor Ushakov found that Ivan Dirikov was simply Ivan Dirikov and wanted only to escape service in Kamchatka and participation in the Bering expedition. Empress Elizabeth, however, showed as much mercy, as if she had found a brother: she had the false bastard packed off to a monastery on double ration.

Later, in the 1740s and 1750s, the false tsars did not even take the trouble to choose names for themselves. These nameless grenadiers simply announced, "People of God, listen to me: I am a tsarevich!"[9] Such shyness invited restraint among the people as well and we do not know of any particular effect those impostors had.

The same cannot be said of those false tsars emerging in the early 1760s; these again assumed the names of past rulers. For clear enough reasons, the new impostors refrained from impersonating Alexis. Two new generations had grown up since the tragic death of Peter I's son, and the name now meant nothing to those who were younger. However fantastic the shapes the false-tsar tales could take and however peculiar the individuals who nominated themselves as pretenders were, they were always careful to have the current false tsar's age more or less match the possible age of a mere mortal. Popular belief, otherwise full of irrational twists as regards such tales was in this respect, imbued with a rather down-to-earth common sense.

Now, if the false-tsar belief needed a fresh medium in those years, it had an ample range to choose from. There had been no less than three sovereigns during the period of palace coups who had passed on the crown quite suddenly, to say the least. Now all three duly returned from the grave.

The first to reappear was Ivan Antonovich, the sixth tsar by that name, impersonated by a monastery peasant called Ivan Matveyev. He sent several letters to the district of Karpogol, promising to topple Empress Elizabeth. He was whipped and exiled into forced labor after his nose was cut off.[10]

The legend concerning Tsar Ivan Antonovich was only at first sight so harmless that Matveyev got off with such a light punishment. In theory the false tsars appearing as Ivan were in a hopeless situation, since the former tsar was still alive. But that was precisely why the gossip and stories around him, abounding in the 1760s, became alarming. Unlike Ivan VI, the new Empress Catherine II had had no genuine right to the throne; she thus had him guarded with extra caution at the castle of Schlüsserburg. This, of course, was not enough to stamp out the rumors around the tsar, who by then had been imprisoned for two decades. This also explains the authorities' over-nervous reaction in 1764 to the unrealistic act of Ensign Mirovich. Correctly labeled a maniac, the officer made a perfectly futile attempt to free the former tsar and help regain his throne. In fact, it was this attempt that gave the guards an excuse to stab the former tsar to death even though he had not known anything about the affair and died innocent of any involvement.[11]

At the same time another false tsar emerged, assuming Peter II's name. Ivan Mikhailov (Yevdokimov) had no desire to harm anybody. He had no dreams of tsardom or any intentions of marching on St. Petersburg. He had only one desire: to taker refuge in a monastery cell, safe among his Orthodox fellows. This can be appreciated even now, knowing that he had been on the run for eighteen years, dodging conscription. His only mistake was to use the false-tsar tale in order to gain a safe refuge. He revealed about himself that, when he had come down with the pox (which was what had killed the original Peter II), the boyars had seized and taken him to Italy. There he had been walled in for twenty-four years, receiving only bread and water from the king. But nine years ago he had managed to escape and had been wandering since from one place to another in the endless plains of Russia.

Yevdokimov was always careful to share his secret only with those from whom he hoped to receive food and lodging. His revelation was successful for a long time, since he had an argument that never failed to convince his Orthodox listeners: he promised to contact the empress in the cause of religious freedom. He was finally undone through the eagerness of a minor clerk who, hoping for a reward, reported to his superiors what he had heard in a village market place about a false tsar hiding in the Nizhegorod district. To the report he appended, interestingly enough, the contents of an overheard conversation of three years before concerning the alleged bastard origins of the real Peter II. The latter item was no longer of interest to the authorities; but the false tsar most certainly was. A verdict was handed down very quickly. Though deserving death, the empress "mercifully agreed" merely to have him whipped in public—in every community where he had fooled people. The government also found it necessary to send an ordinance to the areas concerned. Copies were numbered in order to avoid being read out in places previously ignorant of the affair. Finally, Yevdokimov was locked up in a monastery to the end of his life, and the case was closed—his case but not that of the false tsars.[12]

Already in the same year of 1765, there emerged two impostors pretending to be Peter III, the third male tsar of the era; their example was followed by many impostors over the next two decades. From then on, fraudulent Ivan VIs and Peter IIs were swept away by the flood of false Peter IIIs. Are we facing here another jest by history? How could the Russian people cherish a sovereign who regarded his ascendancy to the Russian throne as a personal tragedy? He who had donned a Prussian military uniform, worn a Prussian decoration and would have done everything to please Prussia and its idolized ruler, Frederick the Great! (Which in fact he did when he withdrew the victorious Russian forces who were battling the Prussians when he came to the throne.) A man who was unable to divest himself of his dolls even as an adult, who had rats hanged after staging court martials, who made terrible faces in church, frightening priests simply because he thought to have found a talent for comedy in himself—why was Peter III so popular?[13]

There is no doubt that Peter III was the most hare-brained tsar in Russian history. The people, however, were unaware of that. All they knew was that a sovereign who neglected the Church of Russia wished to turn ecclesiastical serfs into state peasants and was tolerant to followers of the Old Belief. Thus the "least national" Russian ruler could grow to be a popular tsar among peasants, since he did not live long enough to let the people see him as he really was. Moreover, he was an adult tsar, a fact that was enough to raise the expectation of the masses. It was well-nigh impossible to believe that he could be toppled by a mere wife.

So the rumors that Peter III was still alive started up immediately after his death. Our first document on this is dated May 1763 when a sergeant of St. Petersburg's Ingermansland regiment reported on another for telling him that the sovereign was still alive.[14] This belief lived especially long in the southern territories from which a large number of false tsars had come. Many people supposed the emperor was riding towards Kiev, disguised as a sergeant leading a company of hussars, to settle "the problems of the Ukraine." This is a fine example of the public mood's being most receptive for the emergence of a false tsar.

The first false Peter III came forward as early as 1764.[15] All we know about him is that he worked in the Chernigov territory and, according to the now well-established protocol, was whipped in public at the scenes of his speeches and sent to hard labor for life. The other "Peter III" of that year, a penniless Armenian trader Anton Aslanbekov, was a more interesting character. He forged some documents and fooled people in the Kursk district, introducing himself as a physician at first, then as Tsar Peter. In this latter capacity he was soon arrested, but some déclassé "one-hide-owners" freed their "tsar." In less than half a year he met a similar fate to that of the previous ruler.[16]

The investigation established the number of his followers: he had twenty-three men. Far more, however, fell for one of the following year's false Peter IIIs, a deserter Gavrila Kremniov. In hiding in Voronezh Province, for lack of a better story, he claimed to be a captain bearing extremely good news from headquarters. The role, however, was in sharp contrast with his bare feet; so one of his companions took a look at his dishevelled garments and suggested that he be a tsar instead. Later Gavrila modified this part of his confession, saying he had been so drunk at the time that he could not honestly tell who had had the idea first.

Drunkenness clearly played a major role in his career as a false tsar. One of his most important promises was to allow the making of wine at home, four liters four times a year. Enthusiastically supported by the local priests, he and his followers went from one village to the next. The sequence of events was always the same: the false tsar appeared, the assembled peasants knelt and kissed his hand, then took him to a house where they all drank wine. After lunch there was a ceremonial mass, the people swore loyalty to the impostor, and the party returned to the house to have some more wine. Much wine must have been consumed, the probable reason for the false tsar's having to collect one kopeck per household. In return he promised his followers to suspend head tax for twelve years. We can now see how seriously Kremniov's claim was motivated by his appreciation of good wine, a factor that certainly proved to be a cohesive force among his small but enthusiastic band of followers of at least three hundred resolute men. Of course, their boundless love of drinking was only a part of their motivation. Rather, their support was spurred by attractive promises. Most of these people were one-hide owners, members of that peculiar layer of society between the serving gentry and serfs. Since recent years had increasingly forced them nearer to the latter, they were practically turning into state peasants. They were understandably aggrieved about that and keen to help the false tsars who appeared at the time.[17]

Simultaneously with the thirty-five-year old Kremniov, and almost in the same place, another false Peter III stepped forward, the fourth that we know of that name. (Even their ages were roughly similar: this latter false tsar was thirty-seven, exactly what the genuine Karl Ulrich Peter would have been.) The state in which they announced their "tsarship" (according to all the reports of witnesses, one of total inebriation) was also similar. But Petr Chernishev, also a deserter and from a "one-hide-owner" family, was taken almost instantly when he "revealed his secret." The revelation took place in a village church where the ceremony held at an uncommonly late hour caught the attention of a local ensign who settled the matter straight away. In the now familiar way, Chernishev was whipped and exiled. His punishment, however, did not reform him to the desirable extent; as a convict he proved to be so stubborn that he claimed to be Peter III even in Nerchinsk. A false tsar was obviously in a better position than a thief—he had been flogged as such in the army. Here he received presents from the workers doing hard labor at nearby factories. Nevertheless, in the final account a worse lot fell to him, being exiled even farther—so much farther that he died on the way there.[18]

A common feature of the above false tsars is that each was absolutely insignificant. They were essentially petty impostors; their emergence had nothing to do with politics, consisting of pitiful strings pulled in order to receive a goblet of wine, a small gift or a place to hide. They were not in the least fit for the role of popular leaders. Yet we must not neglect their importance. Some of their ploys would be adopted by Pugachev, the most successful false Peter III; the survival of the legend concerning that tsar would also prepare the ground for him. The example provided by the false tsars already shows that, in a growing number of locations (ranging from the southern territories to the Volga area and to the Urals), a growing number of people were ready to follow a leader as soon as one appeared.

This is why Prince Viazemsky, the chief prosecutor, proved fatally naive in 1767 when suggesting a light sentence for a sergeant who had spread the rumor that Peter III was alive. "The whole world knows already," argued the prince, "that the former sovereign is dead. Therefore, no sane man can believe such an allegation."[19] In the light of the events of the next few years, he would have to ponder much on the question of whether so many madmen could exist even in such a large country.

Chapter 8

A FOLK HERO IN THE
ROBE OF A TSAR

With the mid-seventeenth century, a new era dawned in the history of the Russian peasantry. Until then, partly due to the late and slow development of Russian feudalism and partly because the absolute state built on that foundation reserved the right to subordinate and control all the estates, the Russian peasants were in a relatively favorable situation. They were free to move, had numerous elements of self-government, and a considerable portion of them—the state peasants—were not subject to exploitation by landlords. After the code of 1649, however, the two most numerous social strata in the Russian villages had been undergoing a kind of convergence. The peasants became enserfed when their right to move was revoked. The *kholops* who had the legal status of slaves were also enserfed when Peter I introduced the head tax for all villages to cover the costs of waging war. Although privately the tsar was against the buying and selling of people like cattle, the free disposition of a serf by a master was becoming a standard practice. From that time on, they could be sold, separated from land and family or exiled to Siberia by their owner. As the great Russian thinker Alexander Radishchev puts it in his classic *Journey from Petersburg to Moscow*, Russian peasants had become "talking tools" by the second half of the eighteenth century.[1]

The deterioration in the peasants' position had something to do with the fact that Russia was becoming right then, in the eighteenth century, a monarchy of the nobility. The state was increasingly dependent on the gentry, the former middle layer of the society, granting it a growing number of privileges. This was the first time that the state had passed control over the enserfed peasants to the nobility and, with the exception of a few isolated cases, was never more to involve itself in the private ties between lord and peasant. In the year 1762 the gentry took a further step towards becoming a really privileged class when they were exempted from compulsory state service. That, in turn, left them with enough time on their hands to start "looking after" their serfs—who did not exactly enjoy the process. On the other hand, the idea that the tsar's administration should rescind the service of serfs to their lords, just as it had those of the gentry, began to be expressed. We would not be wrong in assuming that the enlightened Catherine II was deaf to pleas urging her to liberate the serfs.

For one who had corresponded with the French Encyclopedists for example, the tsarina cannot be said to have been reticent. She gave away 850,000 souls during her long reign. Indeed she was especially generous towards her minions. Her charms were substantially enjoyed by Prince Gregory Potemkin, a puller of many strings, the brothers Orlov, who had so obligingly strangled her husband, and a more than adequate amount remained for a number of other admirers. Since their number was high, the presents also strengthened the nobility. We would be unjust, however, if we did not attribute Catherine II's behavior to a conscious policy. Undeniably, she owed much to the guards that had helped her to the throne, and she paid her debt in full to them and, in a broader sense, to the nobility as well. The logical conclusion is that, despite her high-flown ideas and European intellect, she kept the serfs, the vast majority of her subjects, in a form of bondage that was reminiscent of oriental despotism.[2]

It is in the nature of enlightened despotism that a monarch's enlightenment never goes so far as to refrain from sending an

Alexander Radishchev into exile for writing that "the emperor has no clothes," giving voice to the intolerable misery of Russian serfs. The limit of such a monarch's highmindedness is the commutation of false tsars' death sentences to scourging and lifelong hard labor with the initials of the phrase "fraud" branded onto the culprits' foreheads—for humanitarian reasons, which the monarch never failed to advertise. Such a monarch has thus proved that royal mercy has no limits. In 1768, Adjutant Opochinin happened to state that he was Tsarina Elizabeth's son by the king of England. The ensuing investigation made it clear that an ensign called Batiushkov had simply been teasing the young man during a drinking bout. Though the eighteen-year-old boy's father was a general of high reputation, it was generous of the empress to be content with merely transferring Opochinin to border guard service.[3]

Thus, we can see that Catherine II could distinguish between what was important and unimportant. In the latter case she could afford the luxury of being generous. But the cloak of mercy was discarded as soon as her empire was threatened. Such was the case when, after so many petty impostors, a true popular leader assumed the mask of her dead husband, Peter III.

There were, however, still others to try the old sting before Emelian Pugachev led a great popular movement in the guise of Peter III. Before him, in 1773, a Captain Nikolay Kretov claimed to be the former ruler in the faraway town of Orenburg. His motives for the claim were rather prosaic. On his way there from St. Petersburg he had drunk away all his money and was trying to obtain credit from one of the countless resettled exiles by using that little white lie. The magic name was good for only five or six roubles but, according to eyewitnesses, there were several contributors, for the officer ordered his manservant to borrow as much from as many as he could with the tale. The reluctant servant was encouraged by Kretov with the words, "Sooner or later there will be a fool to believe you!" The officer from "St. Petersburg did have the power of prophecy, for some people fell for the story; however, he was reported almost immediately and ended up in prison, where he soon died.[4]

Another type was represented by the false Peter III's working his claim in the previous year of 1772. A fugitive peasant, he enlisted within the territory of the Don host, where unrest was boiling because of the troops that had been transferred there from Moscow. The Cossacks did not quite believe the "tsar" of twenty-five years or so who appeared among them, especially as he bore no facial resemblance to the original. Still, it was a fine opportunity now to teach the gentleman officers from Moscow a lesson. However, one of the captive soldiers found his way to the false tsar's house and solved the problem quickly by slapping "his sovereign" exclaiming, "What sovereign is this?" These words (and even more the act) had their effect on the Cossacks. They themselves delivered the false tsar to Dubovka, then onto Tsaritsyn on the Volga.

Strangely enough, Fedot Kazin Bogomolov (his real name, though sometimes he called himself Kazin) had his greatest success only after being caught. Tsaritsyn was buzzing with the news that the tsar himself was being held captive in the town. The unrest grew day by day until the town's military commander was forced to remove the prisoner to another gaol. In so doing so, he poured hot oil on the fire. The population flooded the street and, upon the false tsar's request, tried to free him. Troops fired into the crowd, which immediately dispersed. The subsequent investigation revealed that there had been a considerable propaganda campaign in support of the false tsar, sweeping beyond the town and reaching across the Volga as far as Kazan; even the Don Cossacks were affected. The situation soon became so delicate that the commander regarded it necessary to replace the whole garrison and sent Bogomolov to Siberia after the usual deterrent punishment. In view of the nervousness of the local authorities, it may perhaps be easily understood why this false Peter III died, just like his prede-

cessor, on his way to exile. But his mysterious death revived the
legends and hopes centered upon his person. Many doubted that
he had died and maintained that he had escaped (now for the second time). The peasants, merchants and soldiers exiled here from
the Volga area, the town's population and the colorful crowd of
vagabonds seeking casual employment along the river thus read-
ied themselves to win Peter III's favor if he deigned to appear
again.[5]

So the time was now ripe not only here, but in the Urals as well.
A large number of factories had sprung up there in the last few
decades. But a vast majority of Russia's industrial workers were
actually serfs ordered by either their lords or the government to
work in the factories. It was sheer slavery; the serfs begged and
begged to be allowed to return to their fields. With the failure of
words action was to follow, and the factory serfs were to find companions in action among the Cossacks of the river Yaik in the Urals.

By the last third of the eighteenth century the absolute monarchy had consolidated itself to such an extent that it was able to take
successful measures to force the population of the periphery, until
then possessors of various privileges, into the despotic system. A
considerable advance in this respect was made in the territory of
the Don host, which the Russian state fully absorbed in the 1770s.
The administration was pursuing a similar policy against the Yaik
Cossacks as well. Their main sources of income, fishing and salt-
making, were declared to be state monopolies. Their hetmans
were appointed directly by St. Petersburg. All the most important
matters that pertained to them were settled by the War College in
the capital. (Previously the tsar had to deal with them through his
foreign office.) At the same time, more and more fortresses were
erected along the border area, ensuring control over one side of the
border as efficiently as defense against the other side. In these
efforts the central government could safely rely on the understanding and support of the Cossack dignitaries.

Theirs, yes, but not that of rank-and-file Cossacks. They had long been simmering over their leaders' "treacherous" behavior and had frequently sent delegations to the capital, begging for the replacement of the current hetman. The answer they most frequently received was a visit by a commission, which could turn into a punitive raiding party at any moment. Thus in January 1772 the commission led by Brigadier General von Traubenberg fired into a crowd of Cossacks assembled at the Yaitsky fortress. The Cossacks then massacred the general and his troops, sent a petition to the empress, begging for mercy and explaining that the other side had opened fire first. To be on the safe side, however, they simultaneously employed the alternative option by declaring war on Russia. The regular troops sent from Orenburg soon silenced them, though. Possibly the authorities did not regard the case to be of great importance, being quite used to such affairs. In the brief period between 1762 and 1769, it had received news of approximately 130 skirmishes with serfs in locations that ranged from the Ukraine to central Russia to as far as the Volga area. Western Siberia was also restless: there the monastery serfs were upset because Catherine II had withdrawn her husband's decree on secularization. On top of this, the ethnic minorities dwelling near the Volga and farther east were in a constant state of unrest. Confident in their power, however, the organs of oppression still felt secure.[6]

This sense of security was to be terribly shaken in the two years beginning with 1773 when, under the leadership of Emelian Pugachev, a fugitive Don Cossack, the scattered minor revolts jelled into a major Cossack and peasant war. Why was this attempt of the Yaik Cossacks more successful than the previous one? The main reason is to be found in the leader and the ideology that, together, bound the movement.

We know a lot about Pugachev's life. He was born about 1742 into an "ancient" Don Cossack family. The life of "simple" Cossacks such as theirs was vastly different than it had been a century earlier. Now these Cossacks either did peasants' work or fought in the imperial armies. Emelian had done his share of both.

He served in the Seven Years' War in Europe between 1756–1763 then was called up again and sent to Poland. This time the Cossacks had the police function of driving back fugitive Old Believers. In 1768 Pugachev served in the war against Turkey, becoming a noncommissioned officer for his bravery. Falling ill, he was allowed to return home. There, however, he could no longer till the land peacefully.

After several unsuccessful attempts, he managed to escape to the Terek Cossacks from where he went on to the Ukrainian and finally to the White Russian Old Believers. Here he learnt of the Yaik Cossacks' revolt and first visited the Volga, then the Yaik rebels themselves, who at the time were in a state of excitement over rumors concerning Bogomolov, the false tsar at Tsaritsyn. At first Pugachev only wished to persuade the local Cossacks to go with him to the Kuban area, then Turkish territory. Later, in a conversation with a Cossack named Pianov, he made a tentative attempt at "revealing" that he was actually Peter III, who had again managed to escape from the prison at Tsaritsyn. Somebody then reported him, and he spent some months in the gaol at Kazan as a fugitive Cossack. In late May 1773 he escaped.

It is difficult to reconstruct the main traits of Pugachev's personality. What follows are the commonplace and factually acceptable characterizations. He was a courageous, good soldier but a restless one. He had seen the world and possessed a rather wide-ranging sense of strategy. But his most important feature was perhaps (as Pugachev himself was to admit later) his extreme ambitiousness: he "had to show himself superior to others." This turned out to have taken roots early; in his youth Pugachev showed his fellows a saber that was supposed to have been Peter I's who, Emelian insisted, had been his godfather.[7]

Gradually, this man of larger horizons found the ideological wonder weapon: the false-tsar story that, in periods of popular unrest and miracle-waiting, had so often had such fantastic results in Russia—when there had been a suitable leader.

It is interesting to follow the gradual shaping, forming and spreading of Pugachev's version. After his escape from prison in Tsaritsyn, the Cossack Emelian Pugachev disappeared forever, to be replaced by Tsar Peter III. The new false tsar made his appearance in August 1773.[8] He was taking a bath at a Cossack manor when his host noticed the scars of an old wound on his chest. Pugachev said it was a tsar's stigmata. His host immediately notified some Cossacks in the neighborhood; they came over and carefully examined their "ruler's" body. Then they asked him many questions, being mostly interested in where he had hidden so long. The "tsar" answered them at length, telling that he had been to Kiev, Poland, Egypt, Jerusalem and, bringing the tale closer to the facts, that he had also visited the Terek and the Don. Finally he "confessed" that he had suffered in prison at Tsaritsyn: thus he identified himself with Bogomolov, the other false Peter III who had served time there—something which was relatively well-known. Thus Pugachev was doubly a false tsar, donning the guise of a previous false Peter III.

Although, after examining the stigmata, the Cossacks declared, "Now we already believe you and recognize you as our sovereign," there is no doubt about those few who were his initial supporters, the innermost core, knew very well with whom they were dealing. One of them stated: "Though he be a Don Cossack and not a ruler, but if he stands up for us instead of the ruler, it is all right with us, as long as he is good for us." Another even explained what the Cossacks expected of him: "...let him bring back the old customs as they used to be and let him finish off all the boyars who are so very cunning in all matters and ruin us."[9]

That was the actual birth of a no-holds alliance. Some desperate men, realizing their troubles and wanting to do something to put them right, chose in effect a leader who echoed their desires. They immediately started spreading the news, carefully playing by the accepted rules of the game. In the night of September 15 there were already about sixty Cossacks, Tartars and Kalmyks assembling at the Tolmachev brothers' manor. Pugachev spoke to them already as a ruler and promised good things to come:

> I am certainly a sovereign. Serve me hon-
> estly and in good faith, and for that I shall
> reward you with the rivers, seas and the
> grass, with money, lead, gunpowder and
> total freedom. I know you all have many
> grievances and you have been robbed of all
> your privileges; but if God gives me the
> tsarship again as He once did, I shall rein-
> state you in your old freedom and ensure
> your well-being.

Two things are clear in this manifesto; at this stage of organizing Pugachev was still insisting on his imperial ancestry, and his main trump argument was the attractive prospect of Cossack freedom.[10]

But the words spoken there were convincing enough to make the number of rebels rise sharply. True, they did not yet feel strong enough to attempt to take the Yaitsk fortress and so they turned north on the river Yaik. In early October they were already at Orenburg and by then the army had 3,000 men and twenty guns. At almost six month-long siege of the fort began. Later it would turn out what a mistake it was for the Cossacks, unfamiliar with siege warfare, to waste time there. Nonetheless all these months were not spent in vain for this was when Pugachev organized his army, instilled military discipline and trained them as well as he could. On November 6 he established his War College which, in addition to army matters, dealt with the everyday management of the territories they controlled. Most important of all, he sent "imperial" ordinances and declarations almost everywhere across the huge land from the Volga to Bashkiria, with the clear purpose of inducing the local population to revolt. Thus the seemingly pointless siege was the initial period for creating a mass base for the uprising.[11]

Those incendiary letters were cleverly written. Among other things, they show that the rebels had a "tsar's chancery" too. They consciously took into account the colorful linguistic, ethnic and social variety of the land around them and wrote each letter in the appropriate language, promising to remedy the specific set of grievances. Naturally, there were a few points common to all these letters. There was always a very short, most often barely factual, account of the "tsar's" miraculous escape. More was written on the causes of the "sovereign's" hardships: he had defended serfs and intended to punish the nobles, so the latter had conspired against him. Obviously, the motive of settling accounts with the nobility could not be left out—though originally Pugachev had considered giving compensation for confiscated land. Some months later, however, the prospect of annihilating the nobility altogether became the dominant idea. The most important part of these ordinances was the promise, sometimes in a general but obviously effective format: "I shall present you with everything you have desired all your lives." But more often there was a detailed list:

> Everybody who had the rank of a peasant earlier and was subordinate to his lord should be our crown's faithful slave and we shall present them with the ancient cross and prayer, with their heads and beards, with independence and freedom and inheritable Cossack status; we shall give them the lands, forests, hay fields and fishing spots and, without taxes, we shall liberate them from the judicial tyranny of mean nobles and cheating town clerks....[12]

A catch-all manifesto indeed! However, it remained silent about how, when it all came true, they would organize that ideal tsarsdom, which would not have nobles—that is, where everybody would be a noble, except the nobles of today, who will not be alive by them. More important was the immediate target—simple and easily comprehensible to everyone—fight the "evil" nobles for the "good" tsar. It is not surprising that it was so successful in such a short time.

In November Pugachev defeated and scattered two imperial relief armies. In the second battle he was already in command of ten thousand men. The success filled the population of vast territories near and far with an enthusiasm that was further enhanced by the military forces the rebel leader sent there. In late 1773 and early in the following year, there was fighting in the Volga and Kama areas as well as in the Southern and Central Urals, Western Siberia, Bashkiria and the Perm region. Skirmishes started even around the Don. Despite the vast territory covered by the general revolt, the main force at Orenburg endeavored to maintain contacts with the isolated movements. In a majority of cases, of course, this meant only that the troops swarming out of Pugachev's camp, and reinforced with local rebels, plunged into independent action which the "tsar" legitimized. Such was the case in Bashkiria where the local commander, Zarubin-Chika, was appointed by Pugachev, who later made him a count. This also demonstrates that "Peter III" was endeavoring to fully exercise the tsar's prerogatives and to follow the customs of the court. This, however, he managed to do only in the most awkward of ways: he granted his man the name and title of the previous commander Chernishev, who had actually been killed by his own Cossacks. Thus, Pugachev created a false count. Later on he was often granting titles and functions, naming the recipients after St. Petersburg courtiers. A false court began to take shape in the style of its false ruler.[13]

Incidentally, this false Count Chernishev acted as the absolute master of Bashkiria. He established his own staff, appointed the commanders of his army, sat in court and passed judgment over those living in the territory under his authority. There were now one or two major rebel armies fighting in every major region, although the real support was provided by the local population, rising in arms everywhere and, where insurgence met with success, establishing organs of popular power, attending meetings and choosing their own hetmans.

This type of warfare is successful only as long as a concentrated attack by regular armies does not take place. Immediately after   St. Petersburg realized the scale of the insurrection and sent strong armies to the affected areas, Pugachev's men were defeated. This was partly due to the false tsar's faulty tactics. By simply awaiting the enemy's arrival, he was practically inactive; in fact he was attending a wedding feast when they did arrive—his own. The marriage he had only undertaken on the request of his closest henchmen, who were beginning to show impatience with their leader's excessive displays of affection for their relatives. Some of them even knew that Pugachev had a wife and children near the Don, thus making the "tsar" guilty of bigamy. The sovereign's prestige fell considerably when his choice fell on a simple Cossack woman.[14]

The wedding was, of course, not the cause of the two consecutive defeats in March 1774 of the false tsar; but these failures sowed the seeds of his army's demoralization. Zarubin-Chika was also defeated and the revolt was over, it might have been thought. Pugachev had only four hundred men left, yet he managed to raise a new insurrection. This success was due to his accurate perception of the situation: leaving Orenburg, he turned towards Bashkiria and the southern Urals, bringing together a number of smaller bonds still fighting there. In May 1774 he was in command of eight thousand men again. The factories of the Urals provided him with a constant supply of arms, so he felt strong enough again to turn west towards Kazan, after which he might have marched unhindered towards Moscow. However, Colonel Ivan Mikhelson's regular army caught up with him and defeated him at Kazan. The scattered rebel army crossed the Volga and, after some hesitation, turned towards the Don. This was the beginning of the third and last phase of this Cossack and peasant war.[15]

Pugachev's luck seemed to hold. The whole of the right bank of the Volga was in revolt. The news of the false tsar's arrival sent people flocking to his camp. Soon Pugachev had twenty thousand fighters, and many of the gentry's houses had been put to the torch by the inhabitants of their estates. Countless cases of incendiary acts were occurring in several central regions: the popular insurrection had reached its most extensive phase. Yet all this contributed to its culmination. The fighting force itself was incomparably weaker than the previous one: barely a few Yaik Cossacks were left beside Pugachev, and both the Bashkirian horsemen and the armories were on the other side of the Volga. Thus the army's breakneck race towards the Don Cossacks (sometimes they covered as many as eighty verst per day) was not without good cause: winning them over would have meant a considerable boost to their fighting capacity.   For the moment the plan worked: the Don Cossacks joined them and the army was besieging Tsaritsyn in August 1774. On the 25th of that month, however, they were again defeated—this time decisively. Pugachev managed to escape across the river to where he had set off the uprising a year before. But by now the Yaik Cossacks' mood had changed; recognizing obvious failure, they decided it would be better to arrest their old leader and hand him over to the genuine authorities.[16]

We could say Pugachev's revolt was doomed to failures. All the leader's skill, all the Cossacks' fighting experience, all the masses' determination, all the mobilizing force of belief in the false tsar proved to be insufficient against a strong army. On closer examination, it can be seen that this popular rebellion, led by the Cossacks, but with a far wider popular base, was a typical peasant rebellion in that it lacked a clear set of objectives; an appropriate level of organization and concentration. Moreover, the "good tsar" faith that had provided the ideological basis was also badly shaken.

Perhaps it all started with Pugachev's setting too much store in insisting on his "genuineness." No doubt his huge movement, consisting of an extremely wide variety of social groups, badly needed to believe in the leader's high birth. That, however, harbored the inherent danger of the leader's becoming a real-life ruler and thus becoming alienated from his people. On the other hand, however hard Pugachev tried to look like a "real" tsar, the results of his endeavors were most doubtful. He took a disproportionate risk whenever he did so. The central government launched an increasingly powerful campaign to prove that "Peter III" was an impostor. That was another reason why the false ruler was compelled to have himself "recognized" by those who did him this favor, but with their own interests in mind. This was obviously a weapon that could backfire at any time.

Even simply playing out the role of a tsar was a risky undertaking for a simple man of Don Cossack stock. However, Pugachev's revolt took place far away from both Moscow and St. Petersburg, in locations where the inhabitants could not be familiar with the tsar and his trappings. To be on the safe side, Pugachev did have his imperial seal, medals and banners and the rest; this seemed to be enough to take the people in. He also endeavored to meet the expectations in other details as well. He acquired a picture of Tsarevich Paul, son of Catherine II and Peter III, and took it everywhere with him as his son's portrait. He even had the nerve to start sobbing in public when the subject of "his son" suffering far away from him emerged in conversation.

Similarly, one of his toasts during drinking bouts was to his son and his son's fiancee.[17] Despite all his caution, he did occasionally make blunders in his role. Once he seated himself on a church throne, which no one other than a priest was supposed to even touch: he thought it was there for the tsar. Those present were shocked, and rumors began to circulate.

As usual, the signs of suspicion increased when the movement was in decline. There were quite a number of symptoms by that time. Everything that could have been a master stroke if success had been achieved, turned against him now. As a false tsar, for instance, Pugachev married beneath his rank and, to make matters worse, his first wife and children turned up in his camp out of the blue. This was not a jealous wife out to make a family scene: she had been invited to Kazan by the central authorities to help uncover her husband; the rebels caught her. "Tsar Peter III" resolved the delicate situation by announcing that the woman was the wife of Pugachev, one of his men who had died a hero's death for him. He thus created a false deceased Pugachev to replace himself. Understandably, this explanation did not satisfy everybody.[18]

Pugachev tried everything. He renamed his fortified villages Moscow, Kiev and so on. He wore a Cossack cap adorned with a golden cross and the star of St. Andrew on his chest all the time. He decorated his entourage with similar medals. Lacking the real Paul, he pondered whether to appoint a false tsarevich or not just to have him in the camp. All these tricks, however, could not overcome basic shortcomings, such as his illiteracy, when faith in his omnipotence was shaken by the military defeats. His prestige as sovereign took a particularly severe blow when he was forced to flee to the Don Cossacks. Nor was it an accident that he had kept away from this area for so long. Many people on the Don recognized their old comrade, and this removed a large chunk of his support. The false-tsar tale was beginning to be a trap, irresistibly seducing the popular leader who had become tsar. Hence he maintained some style in his actual arrest. When he warned the renegade Yaik Cossacks of the consequences of their laying hands on their sovereign, they cynically replied that "If you are really a tsar, you are out of harm's way anyway."[19]

Pugachev was executed on January 10, 1775, after a lengthy investigation interspersed rather hastily, so much so that it was later rumored that he had not really died. Though this was not the main cause, it is a fact that the legend survived, and just as in the time of the false Dmitris, there were new false tsars to step forward into the vacant place of the first.

Pugachev was still alive—indeed, had not even been caught—when another "Peter III" emerged. This was a peasant named Mosyaghin in Tambov province. Though he had not created any particular stir, Count Petr Ivanovich Panin sentenced him to a death. That was designed to deter possible imitators: Mosyaghin was to be quartered then his severed hands, feet and head were to be displayed "at the scene of his crime." True, the "merciful" empress ordered the punishment to be commuted; the governor had soon to report the death of the impostor.[20]

Catherine II displayed far less understanding in this case of a false princess who caused the government in St. Petersburg considerable anxiety during the Cossack and peasant war. In 1772, a beautiful woman of some thirty years of age and with a fluent command of several languages surfaced in Paris; her tale was that she was Tsarina Elizabeth's daughter by Hetman Kiril Razumovsky and she declared her claim on the throne of Russia. Her colorful account included episodes of being exiled to Siberia, receiving aid from the Don Cossacks and learning the secret of her ancestry at the age of seventeen from the shah of Persia. She also claimed that Pugachev, at that time battling imperial authority, was actually her half-brother on their father's side and had assumed Peter III's name in order to topple Catherine II and elevate his sister to the throne. For some years she managed to make a number of influential gentlemen believe her story, facilitated by the fact that the false princess proved to be from imperially distant, demonstrating a heartfelt appreciation of those willing to help her.

She was, however, not taken seriously in politics; a letter from her to the Turkish sultan asking for an army was simply left unanswered. In time her financial sources also ran dry. Catherine II masterfully chose the moment to set her rival a trap. Count Alexis Orlov, who had earlier performed a no less delicate task successfully was chosen to carry out the empress' plan. The cunning courtier prepared the trap for Elizabeth (who had meanwhile moved to Rome) with a stubborn patience. He showed himself to be a consistent and, more importantly, a gallant beau who often helped the "princess" with a friendly loan. In a careless moment Elizabeth was tricked into boarding a Russian ship and was whisked to St. Petersburg. She ended up in the labyrinthine prison of the Peter-Paul fortress. Her plea for an audience with the empress made Catherine II even angrier: "The appropriate measures are to be taken against that wench!" The order was carried out, and within six months the false Elizabeth died in prison.

The identity of this mysterious woman is a question that cannot be answered today. The very existence of the person whose guise she assumed is in doubt. Many experts supposed that Tsarina Elizabeth might indeed have had a daughter sired by Alexis Razumovsky, Kiril's brother and Elizabeth's lover. She was a nun under the name of Dosifeya in the Novospassky convent in Moscow between 1785 to 1810, the year of her death. Her lot, however, was far better than that of a simple nun. The convent received a large annual cash donation. Dosifeya was regularly visited by the patriarch and her funeral was attended by the cream of Moscow society. Her contemporaries must have known more than we do when they paid their last respects to Dosifeya or, as she was known in her previous life, "Princess Tarakanova."[21]

Whether or not the mysterious Princess Tarakanova did have royal ancestry, Catherine found it safer to have her in a convent and the false Tarakanova in prison, or preferably, dead. Catherine seems to have attributed greater importance to the activities of the hot-blooded and politically sophisticated beauty than to the last waves of the great Cossack peasant war. Not that her reasoning was unsound: the individual pockets of resistance, isolated and desperate, were being gradually wiped out. Nevertheless military power was helpless in the face of the legend of resistance.

The imagination of the people proved to be optimistic and inventive yet again: it left no doubt about "Tsar Peter III's" escape from death. Was Pugachev executed?   Well, there were many who failed to believe even that, and those who did failed to lose heart.   Rumors began to circulate that Pugachev and Peter III being two different persons, the former being merely a general of the latter, and after the general's death the sovereign would take the matter into his own hands. According to some other versions, Pugachev's cause would be taken up by Metelkin (Sweeper) a folk hero who would sweep the boyars out of the country.   This messianic legend of Metelkin proved to be so strong that it was still in circulation in the Volga area in the mid-nineteenth century. As usual with legends, this one was also far-fetched in comparison with the actual historical persons who gave it its foundation. What happened was that in early 1775 a military deserter named Ignaty Zemetayev, leading a host of boatmen, attempted to break into the inner territories from the Don. He was crushed at once, but the mere fact of his resistance made his name suitable for keeping up hope in a miracle.[22]

In this general mood it is hardly surprising that there was again somebody to exploit the situation by assuming the name of Metelkin. In 1776 the small landholders of the Yeletsky district revolted and created a false Metelkin for themselves. He encouraged the faint hearted: "Can't you understand, you fools, that it is not me who fights, I am fighting not for myself: it is Tsar fighting through me and he will aid us!"[23]

All in all, this Metelkin belief or another version, fashionable at the time, according to which "Iron Forehead and the Tsar will come and smash the lords," were somehow not the real stuff. With such a stubborn belief in the tsar's survival, sooner or later he was bound to appear in person. It happened as early as the year following Pugachev's death, and the next two decades saw the emergence of at least thirteen more false tsars.[24] All five false sovereigns of the first five years appeared as Peter III; later a Peter II, an Ivan Antonovich and even two Tsarevich Pauls "returned," a fact doubtlessly indicating a gradual loss of appeal and eventual death of the Peter III legend. A similar conclusion can be drawn from the role and importance of the impostors assuming royal identities in these twenty years. We know next to nothing about some of them, since even the most thorough enquires were unable to disclose anything about them beyond the fact that they had misused tsars' names. Their contacts with the population were evidently not of the nature that the government might have found dangerous. On rare occasions, however, some official documents give a few hints on the possible reasons for the impostors' activities. For example in 1776, one Andreyev, a soldier in Narva, a veteran of the Prussian campaign, had sailed to a number of lands, including Malta. He confessed that he would prefer beheading to living in such a poverty as he did. All he requested by his right of "royal birth" was to be allowed to go to Holstein, his "native land." The false-tsar story he span was to help a globe-trotting soldier to depart for abroad. Others had even more prosaic reasons. The peasant smallholder Gerasim Savelov in Kursk province wanted to raise money for his wedding. He managed to get possession of a blue coat on the Kola peninsula and paid for it by laboring to the end of his life.[25]

The Don Cossack Maxim Hanin can be considered the most significant impostor of the period, though even his case demonstrates the inevitably pitiful nature and futility of the false-tsar venture in the years following the crushing of Pugachev's revolt. Hanin's fall was due to his fondness for young girls. At the time the Volga Cossacks were exiled from Dubovka in retaliation for their role in the "mutiny," and their place had been taken by new settlers. One of them, a peasant, had brought his pretty daughter of eighteen along.

On one occasion the father went to settle some affairs, leaving his child alone at home. One day in February 1780 a priest and his son entered the house, accompanied by two peasants, and forced the girl to leave with them. Some days later they reassured the returning father, telling him what a great honor befell him: his daughter had been taken to Peter Fyodorovich. To be on the safe side, they also promised the father that his son would be allowed to leave the army and return home. However, the peasant Prokhorov was not impressed and turned to the authorities. The daughter was ordered to be set free and questioned. Her testimony gave a curious twist to abduction. It turned out that her fifty-year-old abductor had "revealed his secret" to her at a most intimate moment, saying something along the lines that "It is not just any man you are lying with, it is Tsar Peter III himself!"

Even that had failed to impress the girl, who also disclosed that many peasants and Cossacks had come to visit the "tsar," whispered with him, called him "batiushka" and sovereign, and forced presents on him. Next the culprit was questioned. He said he was Maxim Hanin, a Don Cossack with a stormy life behind him. He admitted violating the girl but denied committing any other crime. The investigation went on at full tilt and brought results. According to the discovered details, the turn in Hanin's life had come in 1778 when he had met Oruzheynikov, an old comrade of his from the rebel army at Samara. The aging roué had had a low opinion on the whole uprising and had never seen Pugachev. Accordingly, on their way out of a pub he had asked his drinking companions, "What was that famous Pugachev like?" Oruzheynikov had looked at him before answering, "He looked just like you."

The idea took hold immediately. Oruzheynikov made it even more attractive by telling Hanin that the army in the Urals was waiting only for a leader to appear and lead them against Moscow, then to St. Petersburg. Hanin did not simply wait for that day, for in many villages in the Don area he tried to convince the population of his high origins. The abduction of the girl put an end to his aspirations. The false tsar was transferred to Samara and is never mentioned in the records again. There can be little doubt his fate.[26]

This budding affair that might have had some effect on the people was crushed before it could really begin. There is even less to be said about the other false tsar—perhaps the only one

among them to achieve considerable support was Kondrati
Selivanov, leader of an Old Believer sect of fanatics, the *skoptsy*.
Among the faithful he enjoyed the measure of respect due to a
deity. Everybody regarded him as a future redeemer and shrouded him with a mystical haze. Though he assumed Peter III's name
after being exiled to Siberia, this was but a kind of extra pedigree,
as his followers did not expect him to save him in his capacity as
tsar. In 1796 he was locked up in a lunatic asylum.[27]

This took place at the same time as the last Peter III emerged.
The legend itself lived much longer; as late as in 1900, the Ural
Cossacks maintained that Pugachev and Peter III had been the
same person. The passing of time, however, did not favor the
adoption of that name by false tsars. As a peculiar development,
the brightest career among the many false Peter IIIs took place
outside Russia, in Montenegro, where Stepan Maly took power
through the tale and held it from 1767 until 1773.[28] The very
number of false rulers after Pugachev in Russia also shows their
insignificance and an inflation of the false-tsar belief. The people
were weary, while the institutions of oppression firmly maintained. Indeed the establishment could now afford the luxury of
refusing to take these impostors seriously and, in the spirit of
enlightenment, declare them insane. After quartering, whipping
and lifelong hard labor, the typical punishment for the offense was
now the insane asylum. This alone demonstrates the speedy decline
in the importance of the false-tsar concept.

Chapter 9
THE LEGEND DIES

The arrival of Paul I on the throne was the death blow to the Peter III belief, already in its last throes. A new tsar came to reign, and as usual, people awaited him with high expectations and hopes. Thus there was no need for new false tsars to emerge, as the people expected the legitimate one to make their wish come true. This is proved by the 1,205 petitions that arrived on his desk in the first three months of his reign. Most of these requested their authors to be ascribed again as state peasants.

Needless to say, the Little Father failed again to realize his subjects' dreams. Indeed, he was hardly capable of doing so, as he was psychotic by the time he came to the throne. The distortions of his psyche were caused by the fact that he (supposing, of course, that his father really had been Peter III which even he doubted) had a better claim to the throne than his mother Catherine, who gained it illegally. Consequently, the "enlightened" tsarina had always kept a special eye on her son, surrounding him with a network of informers and repeatedly warning him to wait his turn peacefully. The tsarevich had to wait uncomfortably long, until he was forty-two years old, by which time his nerves had gone to shreds in the atmosphere of constant suspicion and distrust. And he had had good reasons to feel insecure, as his mother had constantly threatened to shut him out of succession, which then would go to her grandson, the future Tsar Alexander, Paul's own son. Paul's habit of placing a double guard around his residence at Gatchina and along the road to Tsarskoye Selo where his mother spent the summer every year was thus not at all an extreme measure. Catherine was well aware of the fact that the people were expecting much from not only her dead husband, but from her still-living son.

Finally, the tsarevich became tsar and nothing happened to improve the lot of the masses. Naturally, the lot of some improved since out of hatred for his mother, Paul pardoned many exiled and imprisoned persons. Otherwise there was no change; indeed things actually became worse because the paranoia of the ruler had an adverse effect on foreign politics. There was only one area in which the tsar remained consistent—the position of the serfs. Not only did he fail to cut the number of landowners' serfs, he actually increased it. Within four years he transferred to the nobility almost as many state peasants as his mother had done in thirty-four years. The petitioners were whipped. Revolts were crushed.[1]

It is not surprising that there was no grief when he met an end similar to his father's in 1801. This was the last palace coup in the history of Russian tsars. The similarity to the previous one is striking: the tsar's son, Alexander gave his blessing to the plot, just as the previous tsar's wife, Catherine, had done. The only difference was that it had been relatively easy to strangle Peter III with a belt; his son, however, fought like a cornered rat and was hacked to death in his bedroom only after a lengthy struggle. That unworthy death was a fitting end to an unworthy reign.[2]

This makes it understandable why Tsar Paul failed to come back from the dead after 1801. Though two people assumed his name while he was a tsarevich, he gave us only one false tsar and that no closer than far off Siberia. However, this Afanasy Petrovich, "Tsar Paul," kept working on the population of Siberian villages for two decades. His long stint ended when a supporter at Krasnoyarsk took the matter into his hands and wrote to Tsar Alexander himself, informing him that the stigmata on his protégé's body seemed to prove that the the man in the simple attire was His Majesty's father. Since the culprits could not be sent any further off into exile, a Solomonic verdict was born: the correspondent was forbidden to employ the services of the imperial post office ever again.[3]

The false-tsar belief then had a hiatus for a few decades. Its absence was in obvious connection again with the hopes concerning the new sovereign. These seemed to have serious bases, for in the initial period of his reign Alexander I did indeed make a tentative attempt to introduce some reforms or at least toyed with the idea of reforms. Had these been carried out, these would not have served the interest of those who would have been affected. Even the peasants, who had an initial trust in each new tsar, could sense that. This is the background to the most extraordinary event in the history of the Russian social conscience, when some people built their hopes for a short time (1805–1807) on a foreign ruler—Napoleon, of all people.[4]

In 1807 a peasant was imprisoned in the Peter-Paul fortress for spreading the news that Napoleon had called on the tsar to liberate the serfs, threatening war otherwise. Documentary evidence shows that this rumor was especially widespread among the peasants in the vicinity of St. Petersburg. Nothing more than an interesting episode, the expectations around Napoleon dissipated in the 1812 war. A sense of patriotism had by this time rejected the notion of Napoleon as redeemer and replaced it with that of Napoleon as Antichrist. At the same time, this reborn patriotism worked against the false-tsar ideology: the need to rally around the flag to a foreign invasion diminished domestic tensions.[5]

1825 was the year when certain events proved to be sufficient to revive the seemingly dead belief in false tsars. This was the year when Tsar Alexander died suddenly under mysterious circumstances in the town of Taganrog after a rule of two-and-a-half decades. Later he was reported to have ridden his horse for four hours in an icy wind and to have caught a bad chill; as he had never had any serious illness, his death came as a surprise to everyone. It happened far away from the capital, and it took some considerable time for the corpse to be delivered back to St. Petersburg, where the coffin was left unopened. In Taganrog, however, some of those who had seen the tsar's body insisted that it had looked most unfamiliar. In these unusual circumstances, many were quick to recall Alexander's frequent promises to abdicate. Even his words to his brother Nicholas received a special significance: "How glad I should be to see your procession march before me in the street and I, one of the crowd, just wave my cap and shout hurrah!"[6]

Inevitably the rumor started to make the rounds that the tsar had not died but retreated from the vanities of this world. This proved to be so strong that even the future Tsar Nicholas II was not entirely convinced of its falsity. Some historians confirm the likelihood of a feigned death, referring to a number of indicators, including the increasing number of international (the dissolution of the Holy Alliance) and domestic (secret societies) problems which may have rocked the self-confidence of a tsar whose disposition was in any case rather shaky. They argue further that Alexander had long been ridden by guilt and remorse for having his father murdered. He was also deeply affected by the death of his much beloved illegitimate daughter Sophia.

A full decade later something happened to feed those rumors and strengthen idle speculation into firm belief. On September 4, 1836, a dignified, respectable-looking man appeared in the Krasnoufimsk district of the province of Perm. He was wearing peasant clothes but riding a majestic-looking horse, which caused him to be arrested right away as a suspicious character. Under interrogation, the white-bearded old man's name turned out to be Fyodor Kuzmich, and that was all he remembered about himself. The scars of a whipping on his body bore witness to an eventful past. Just for good measure, he received the same treatment here as well and was then exiled as a vagabond to Western Siberia. Fyodor Kuzmitch heard the sentence announced with obvious satisfaction.

The mysterious stranger found haven in the province of Tomsk but instead of retiring to an outlying monastery, he kept up active contacts with the inhabitants. All the locales looked on the straight-backed old man with an interest and awe that increased as time went by. Soon everybody knew that the man who had surfaced among them in the middle of nowhere was no ordinary man. Fyodor's incredibly wide range of knowledge, his education, command of languages and whole attitude imbued his peasant audience with wonder. Those who saw and heard him had no doubt that they had encountered a very high nobleman. Their conviction was only made stronger by Kuzmich's refusal to ever say anything about his origins. Whenever the subject arose, he always brushed it aside with some hazy generalities. News of him soon reached Tomsk, and a rich merchant named Hronov invited the old man to live with him. On his estate, four versts from the town, he had a small house built for this vagabond of the noble looks, who lived there in ease compared, of course, to the conditions prevailing thereabouts.

Fyodor Kuzmich died a very old man in 1864 on the estate of Hromov, the merchant, and took the secret of his identity with him to his grave. Yet the secret was considered an open one even during his life by a large number of people, who were unshakably convinced that he could be none other than the Tsar Alexander who had disappeared in Taganrog. The legend slowly took shape and grew stronger, so much so that even some historians were reluctant to exclude the possibility. Several eyewitnesses stated that Kuzmich looked exactly like the tsar. The old man himself maintained his mysterious silence concerning his identity to the end.

Could Fyodor Kuzmich and Alexander I be the same person? For an answer, the particulars of the question have to be examined. Can it be proved that Alexander I did not die in 1825? It seems unlikely that it can since the allegedly dead tsar was seen both in Taganrog and on the way to St. Petersburg by many people who did not dispute his identity. Did Fyodor Kuzmitch exactly resem-

ble the tsar? Even this seems to be contraindicated by the fact that
Kuzmich was 171 centimeters tall, while according to some records,
the tsar was much taller than that. Last but not least, knowing the
character of the tsar, can he be supposed to have gone into voluntary exile?[7]

Alexander I was greatly pharisaical, but his unbalanced mental
state, his sudden changes of mood and opinion must have been
caused by a basic duality in his character. In theory, therefore, it
is possible that he reached a state of mind in which he grew tired
of his miscarried attempts at reforms, became fed up with the oriental despotism that filled the bottom of his heart with fear and
despair and ran away out of a sense of guilt for his moral double
standard. Whether he would have chosen the method of retreat
from the world that Fyodor Kuzmich did is hardly likely, however. His life in the years 1825 to 1836: — several public whippings
and fanatical penitence in total anonymity — would signify a character too spiritual to have been Alexander I's. But even then, sup-
pose the tsar did have the powers of a saint (for which nothing in
his long reign provides evidence). How then can the sharp change
in his behavior after 1836 be explained? How to account of this
constant exhibitionism in the hope of free meals, this provincial
grand seigneur style, this pitiful role-playing? These two phases
of a supposed voluntary retirement point to two totally different
personalities.[8]

Thus we need a more plausible explanation for Fyodor
Kuzmich than identifying him as the tsar. He was perhaps indeed
some high-brow aristocrat (some are inclined to identify him with
a noblemen called Uvarov) whipped and exiled for a serious
crime, perhaps to Kamchatka, as hinted at by Uncle Kuzmich during one of his hazy "confessions." After many years he managed
to escape and got as far as Krasnoufimsk. After Kamchatka it
must have been a relief only to be exiled as a nameless tramp to
western Siberia, where he succeeded in settling down comfort-
ably. Fyodor Kuzmich's display in Tomsk makes it far more like-

ly that we have here a very clever impostor who simply sought material gain. He was somewhat similar to the Kretov-type false tsar but with the difference that the old man was wiser than his fellows. He never risked claiming to be a tsar but, through his curious vagueness, never excluded the possibility of the highest origins, cleverly contributing to the establishment and spread of the legend around his person. In the end he achieved the same results as if he had claimed to be the ruler while managing to minimize the risk.[9]

That risk was twofold. There was the usual retribution on the part of the authorities, and interestingly, there was the threat of vengeance by non-official Russia. We must remember that in the last phase of his reign Alexander I showed his true character making the masses stop regarding him as a good tsar. Hardly anyone could have gained an advantage from assuming Alexander I's name; indeed, aside from Fyodor Kuzmich's cautious venture, no one else attempted to do so. Despite the tsar's indeed mysterious death, it inspired no false tsars.

Curiously enough, the emergence of new false tsars was aided by another event in the year 1825. This had, if possible, even more to do with the Taganrog affair, as it concerned the succession. In the event of Alexander's death his brother Constantine would have been first in the line of succession, followed by the other brother Nicholas. However, in 1820, Constantine renounced all his rights of succession in favor of his younger brother. Thus Nicholas became the heir apparent, but the population knew nothing of this, as Constantine's decision was not publicized. Consequently, after November 19, 1825, the authorities began administering loyalty oaths to Constantine, as they were required to do. The beneficiary of those oaths, however, did not hasten to confirm his decision, and thus Nicholas's coronation was not the smooth affair it should have been. Hardly a month after Alexander's death, it became necessary to take again people's oaths of loyalty, this time to Nicholas. That had two important consequences. One was the emergence of the Decembrists who chose that very day, December 14, to launch their uprisings. They also wished to ride the wave created by an "illegal" succession.[10] Even more important than the Decembrists, the other consequence was the people's reaction to a show that was understandably strange to ordinary people. For them, Nicholas's tsarship was "false" because of the suspicious circumstances in which there was a "genuine," rightful candidate Constantine, for tsar. The conditions were thus ripe for the circulation of wild rumors about the grand duke. He was supposed to be approaching via Narva with three divisions, according to one version, to kill the ruler. In another version, the tsar had him imprisoned in the Peter-Paul fortress. Some spread the news that he had been wounded by the lords; others seemed to know he was riding near Kiev. Still others named Korea, Turkey, France or some other country as the place where he fled. All these stories had one thing in common: the fact that they expressed and embodied the people's expectations concerning Constantine, in a way that could be expressed as "Seeing his barbaric disorder in Russia, the burden of despotism and suppression on simple people, he intends to change these things as soon as possible." Though the real grand duke was far from liberal, a legend slowly started to envelop Constantine similar in nature to the early Russian redeemer legends.[11]

After tracing two centuries of Russian false tsars, we know that in a situation where such beliefs are institutionalized, the "redeemer" himself will inevitably appear sooner or later. The first emerged as early as Christmas 1826 in the province of Saratov. A veteran Korneyev appeared twice more in neighboring villages before the end of the following to year. Korneyev obliged all his followers to guard his secret. This was understandable, since the real Constantine was still alive. Eventually the "grand duke" was duly reported.[12]

Then Constantine died in the 1831 cholera epidemic. This the people refused to believe, and as if on schedule, the second false grand duke came forward in the province of Tambov. But the greatest number of rumors concerning Constantine circulated in Siberia. Unlike the two previous false Constantines arrested here, the one caught in 1835 found considerable support among the inhabitants of the province of Yenisey. After promising to cut the head tax, this hussar deserter called Nikolay Protopopov was given food and horses by the Siberians, and the police had great difficulty catching him.[13]

For the sake of variety, two women claimed to be the late grand duke's widow and sister, respectively, in 1831 and 1833. They were not the least disturbed by the facts that Constantine Pavlovich's wife had died earlier and Maria Pavlovna had married and gone to Weimar decades before. Investigation revealed that the false Maria was insane. The rest of this decade passed without either false dukes or rumors. The next impostor emerged in 1840 in the province of Viatka and tried to prove his high birth by displaying the stub of his missing left forefinger.[14]

The case occurring in 1845 was perhaps the only significant one, as regards the possible consequences. Its importance derived from the events of the preceding years. The head of the Ministry of State Domains, Count Paul Kiselev introduced some reforms on government estates from 1838–1840. Those reforms would have meant some relief for the local peasants, but they were accompanied by an incredible amount of bureaucratic interference and, worse still, some additional taxation. Those affected understandably protested. At first they expected the tsar to withdraw his evil minister's decrees, then they hoped for the heir to the throne to help them. Finally and because of the foot dragging by those two, they began to issue manifestoes. In the end the affair ripened into open revolt. There were forty thousand who took part around Chelyabinsk and similar events took place in other areas as well.[15]

Strangely enough, the false-tsar belief did not come into play to assist the revolt; only after it was mercilessly crushed did the victims turn to it. The peasants clung stubbornly to their conviction that the current state of affairs was abominable and a higher power would put things right sooner or later. They were forced to realize that Tsar Nicholas was not going to be their redeemer. The rumor then flared that Grand Duke Constantine was on his way there to investigate the case. This took solid shape in 1845. In the province of Orenburg people started talking about a man visiting villages sometimes in peasant, sometimes in Cossack garb and telling the peasants that he had left his army on the Kirghiz plains, from where he would lead them to teach a cruel lesson to both the officials and those peasants who had refused to join the rebels in 1843. This piece of news even appeared on the agenda of village assemblies. In the village of Gorokhovaya, a self-appointed prophet named Ivan Klyukin insisted that this mysterious person must be Constantine himself and claimed that he had incontrovertible evidence for this. They had taken a bath together and he had had the opportunity to view the other man's chest. Miraculously, the hair on the man's chest was in the shape of the cross! After a large number of arrests, it turned out that the hairy-chested false tsarevich was indeed Constantine, through Kalugin not Romanov, and was an exile, not a grand duke.[16]

Typically medieval in content and form, this example of the belief seems to be a rather late one in the mid-nineteenth century. It occurred in faraway Siberia: the false tsarevich and the peasant movement were unable to form an alliance. These two taken together seem to suggest a slow fading of the false-tsar belief. This seem to be confirmed by the fact that there was no recurrence for some time after 1845; the concept was no longer making a splash. However, this would be to underestimate its attraction. With awe-inspiring regularity it returned to fascinate the imagination of the masses.

Inevitably perhaps, the last upsurge before it petered out completely was in connection with the 1861 serf reforms. Peasants had earlier reacted to every single measure taken in order to "settle" their lives. Although all these solutions had been unfavorable to them, they had always maintained their illusions on their tsar, even if the only way they could do so had been through the false-tsar variation on the "good-tsar" belief. This was the case with the manifesto of February 19, 1861, which "remedied" the problem of Europe's most backward system of serfdom in a way that was not at all to the taste of the oppressed serfs. Its failure to do so can be seen by the approximately two thousand minor peasant rebellions that were intended to inform the new tsar, Alexander II, that his evil officials had abused his obviously ideal royal ideas.[17]

In some cases people expected the revival of the Constantine legend to drew attention to the great difference between the noble aim and its disappointing implementation. They hoped the grand duke would see to things and inform the tsar on the true state of affairs. It would be difficult today to decide which Constantine was to be assigned by the people to such duty: the tsar's dead uncle or the tsarevich by that name. What can be stated firmly is that the expectations around Constantine started anew in 1861. Several false tsareviches emerged in several areas, the provinces of Perm and Saratov being two of those affected.[18]

However, because of the greater-than-ever trust in the genuine sovereign, they were of no real significance, even in the seemingly favorable climate of peasant protest. This time the false-tsar belief had finally and at last lost its primacy among the ideologies of social resistance and was replaced again by the unconditional "good-tsar" concept. This is proved dramatically by the Bezdna case.

The peasants of that village wanted to interpret the Emancipation Act of 1861 as a revolution rather than a reform. In this spirit they claimed that, from then on, every plot of peasant land was free, and those who denied this had been bribed by the landowners. Anton Petrov, their leader, scraped together all the elements of faith in the "good tsar" to rouse his fellow peasants out of their stupor. He showed them a book in which, he said, it was written down that now they would have total freedom. Should they fail to understand that within three months of grace, the tsar would withdraw the decree for which he had suffered enough.

Later events showed that Petrov was anything but naive; in fact, he just the opposite. Familiar with his fellows' way of thinking, he consciously elaborated the appropriate tale. His incendiary speeches left little doubt that they would have to endure much suffering, as the winning of liberty would not be automatic. He foretold the arrival of soldiers who would shoot at them and Christian blood flow of. But he reassured the peasants that the tsar would not leave it at that and would not allow bloodshed. The soldiers would not fire more than three times because he, Petrov would walk up to the commander and then would be carried off to the tsar from whom he would return bearing the manifesto that would put everything right.

It was as if Anton Petrov had written the script for the events that followed; everything happened as he had prophesied. Armed soldiers arrived and opened fire on the crowd. The people stood patiently, shouting only "the tsar's blood is flowing! You have shot the tsar himself." Then Petrov stepped forward, raising high the book which he hoped would stop the solders' firing. They did hold their fire. At this point reality took over. The leader of the Bezdna rebels was arrested but that did not help their cause. Rather than compensating them for their sufferings, the "good tsar" increased them by having the rebels cruelly punished.[19]

Thus the leading ideology of the peasant movements following the 1861 reform was the old belief in a "good tsar." This is perfectly understandable, for something really did happen for the benefit of peasants, and they were inclined to attribute it to the sovereign, the tsar liberator. At the same time, with the reflex of tradition, they blamed the high officials, the *chinovniki,* for their grievances in connection with that decree. In a situation like this, the false-tsar tale as a belief system in the struggle against the lawful tsar was evidently not popular. When it did come into effect, however, it underwent a change of function, becoming a supportive, auxiliary element of the "good-tsar" belief. The last variation

Smick

on the theme of the false-tsar legend is its absorption by the faith
in a "good sovereign." This return to square one is not surprising,
since the false-tsar legend emerged out of naive monarchism
about two-and-a-half centuries earlier and had never ceased to be
an aspect of the illusions concerning the tsar ever since then.

This, however, was not the only factor in its inevitable disappearance by the second half of the nineteenth century. Nor was it
even the main cause. The point has been made repeatedly that
several preconditions were necessary for the emergence of false
tsars, whose most productive periods were generally related to the
great Cossack and peasant movements. But such major movements were not to recur again in Russia until 1905. Revolts, of
course, were not the indispensable conditions for the appearance
of false tsars. The really indispensable conditions was the sudden
death or disappearance of a member of the tsar's family, unless
that member had earned a bad reputation. Nevertheless, after the
1860s no tsar or tsarevich suited those conditions.

Another point is that the false-tsar belief, generally speaking,
presupposed a low cultural level among the masses of people. But
the slow, controversial and rudimentary start to capitalist development beginning with the 1861 reform started, in a sense, spreading the most widely differing achievements of civilization en
masse. The railway, telegraph, newspapers brought even the
remotest corners of the gigantic empire closer to the capital. The
false-tsar belief had been characteristic of the outlying areas even
in the eighteenth century. In the nineteenth, the belief was pushed
to even the remotest corners until this form of fraud became easily detectable and thus impossible to pull off.

Not that there were no more impostors claiming to be tsareviches, for some isolated cases do occur later. However, it is clear
that the false-tsar belief ceased forever to be the driving belief
behind popular discontent. Self-appointed tsars found no support,
and their sole motive became to take advantage of people. This is
true even if contemporary Russian revolutionary movements did

make use of the legend in the hope of mobilizing the people in the way it had been traditionally done. The well-worn "good tsar" tale was used by the Narodniks who "went to the people" and tried to rouse the masses for the revolution by employing the tsar's name, as they did in Chigirin in 1875. Even in the mid-1870s, these desperate revolutionaries did not refrain from appointing one of themselves as Constantine to have the false grand duke make the responsive masses see reason. Their failure shows again that the concept had lost its essence and ossified into an empty form. The people's ideology of a "redeemer" had thus gradually became an impostor's trick, a confidence men's story.

Even in that quality it could not aspire for exception. Rather, we can say it was replaced by a popular epidemic of abusing and exploiting any title or rank. In a manner of speaking, the false tsars had come down to earth and started feeding more innocent stories to the population. What had earlier been dangerous to the existing social order now sank to the level of common crime. The successors to false tsars who had once set out against Moscow had far more modest targets now: a free journey down the Volga, replacement horses at post stations and, of course, money and small favors. Their lies were in proportion to their demands. Most of those impostors pretended to be only lower-ranking princes and counts or took on the identities of physicians, army doctors, judges, attorneys, registrars or auditors. From Gogol's *Inspector General,* we have a fully drawn picture of these Hlestakovs. The contemporary press provides the best proof of how common impersonation had become. Reports abounded about the surprisingly witty tricks pulled by a multitude of false auditors, minor and major functionaries and the like.

This example from 1892 provided mirth to the inhabitants of Samara and Saratov. A steam boat was passing up the Volga at full speed when it was stopped by a barge. The suspicious-looking characters came on board at twilight. They claimed to be secret agents, listened to the captain's report, had a substantial dinner and retired to the first-class cabin obligingly offered to them. While they slept, the news went round at lighting speed among the passengers that those important dignitaries had surely arrived to check on the transport along the Volga; no one, however, dared to ask them for obvious reason. Their ungentlemanly looks were, according to the passengers, part of their meticulously prepared disguise. On waking up, the the two impostors were so much carried away by their success that they commandeered a government ship and had themselves taken to Saratov. Typically, even when they were under strong suspicion after brawling with each other on board, no one had the courage to ask them for identification. They were finally uncovered when someone shouted "Attention!" and one of them, an army deserter, instinctively came to attention.[20]

The following year's most telling case was that of a peasant named Butirin. One day two official-looking strangers visited him. One of them announced that they were bringing him a summons to the court at Samara. The hospitable peasant invited the two "officials" into his house and was about to light the fire under his samovar when the guests demanded "something stronger." Then, stamping their feet heavily on the floor, they forced him to sign the paper and reward them for their labors. The fifty roubles demanded set the peasant thinking, but it was the seal that roused his suspicions. When he timidly asked why it was so small, the chief chinovnik informed him that "Small cases need small seals!" This was all very well; but the amount demanded was enormous for Butirin, who was totally shocked by the contrast between the tiny seal and the large sum. He gathered his courage and ran to the authorities at night. The two impostors were arrested. They turned out to have used possibly the simplest materials, the brass buttons of a school uniform and some blank court forms.[21]

Another case in Tomsk in those years was far more ambitions. One day the local police chief received a telephone call from the local Hotel Europe. A most annoyed voice angrily asked why nobody had organized an official reception for him, Prince Shirinsky-

Shikhmatov, the prosecutor from St. Petersburg. In order to avoid even more trouble, the embarrassed police chief hastened to draw up an ambitious program for his grace. The prince visited the local university, wrote a few friendly words into the guest book and listened to the annual report. Then he accompanied the fire brigade to a call, after which he praised the firemen and rewarded them five roubles. He ended up in prison when his name turned out to be Maurin. He had assumed the prince's identity simply because he wanted to travel free from Saratov to Tomsk. In that he was successful.[22]

On the surface these cases have very little in common with the classical false-tsar affairs; yet they are shockingly similar to those of the second echelon of royal impostors who had always been present behind those self-appointed rulers with political inclinations and gradually overwhelmed them. In exploitation of the popular psyche, the above cases are typical of abuses under any name. Yet in these simple tricks, however, we can see the consequence of a way of thinking: unreserved respect for a name and title, fear of those who represented power, cowering before any authoritative attitude or a strident voice. These reactions are known to other peoples as well; here, however, these were anomalies of social life.

The false-tsar faith then ceased to act as the most dangerous enemy to polity after a remarkably successful run spanning two and a half centuries, featuring so many breathtaking triumphs and dazzling successes. Once it raised a tsar to the throne, brought hundreds of thousands of people under its banner, held tens of thousands in terror. But, however many times it had shaken an empire to its foundations, its operation had still been based on cheating, fraud and lies. All that was left to our time is the Ostap Bender type of swindler.

Chapter 10

FROM TSAR GRISHKA
TO OSTAP BENDER

We are coming to the end of the history of false tsars that flooded Russia in three great waves: those of the Dmitries in the seventeenth, the Peter IIIs in the eighteenth and the Constantines in the nineteenth centuries. In following their careers, we have already mentioned some of the laws under which this phenomenon occurred. It may be worth taking stock of them again.[1]

It has been clear since the first chapter that our focus has been mainly on the political and socio-historical aspects of the problem. The starting point is that the period between the early seventeenth and mid-nineteenth centuries can be seen as a homogenous phase of development in the history of the Russian peasantry, and accordingly, the historical, socio-psychological and ideological foundations for this belief-system were more or less uniform. It is therefore no accident that the false-tsar belief had just as lively a career in the early seventeenth century as in the mid-nineteenth. The upper and lower limits of the period separate these two and a half centuries into sharply different periods. The capitalist development beginning with the 1861 reforms is well known to have opened a new period in Russian history. Likewise a new period opened in the Russia of the late sixteenth century: the age of neo-serfdom. In the events that spilled a sea of blood in the early seventeenth century, the Russian peasants reacted precisely to their changed living conditions, and the immediate mobilizing force for their movement was the false-tsar belief. In addition to the convergence of favorable accidental events, its main cause can be regarded as lying in the fact that tsardom in Russia was a new institution (the first tsar, Ivan IV was also the first "good tsar"); in its ascendant phase. An institution blessed by the Orthodox Church, it was too strong to be attacked. Later, with the consolidation and increasing harshness of serfdom, the oppressive institutions of the political system based on perpetual serfdom were being refined. Of the great popular movements in Russia, beginning in the last third of the seventeenth century, major rebellions took place only in the most outlying areas of the country, the intervals between them grew increasingly longer, and after Pugachev's revolt in the last third of the eighteenth century, they practically ceased until 1905.

We must bear all this in mind when trying to interpret the false-tsar phenomenon, since the false-tsar belief (as it has been made clear) was in close connection with all the different expressions of the current social conflicts; in its capacity as one of their ideological mainstays, it usually followed the movement of popular resistance. Here, however, we must impose several limitations. First, the false-tsar faith was not the one and only ideological creed of social conflict in Russia, whereas the "good-tsar" belief remained a dominant feature throughout the whole period under survey. The false-tsar faith was a variation on the "good-tsar" belief, its most radical variation—the purpose of which was to legitimize the struggle conducted against the good tsar himself. This is the feature which helps shed some light on the people's way of thinking, which made it so difficult to break away from tradition. It demonstrates that popular insurrection against traditional order copied its ideological system from the very order it was fighting to topple.

Second, we must note that the false-tsar ideology had a life of its own. This means that once devised, the false-tsar idea did not have to be rediscovered for every occasion; latent faith needed only to be strengthened with new "proof" adopted to the actual circumstances. On the other hand, it also means that a popular movement could be significant (as Bulavin's revolt in Peter I's time) even if the other necessary conditions for recreating the legend of the redeemer were missing. Some of these conditions were related to a measure of truth, however small, to be necessarily present in the current legends. The false-tsar legend could revive only when a tsar died under really mysterious circumstances, possibly after a very short tenure on the throne, or was murdered outright. (It was even better if he were succeeded by a woman.) Nevertheless, even this was insufficient if the tsar reigned too long or had managed to earn a bad reputation among his people even within a short period. On the other hand, the people always gave their confidence to a new tsar; therefore, "false-tsarhood" was mostly suspended or at least considerably weakened in the initial period of every tsar's reign. Another point is that, unlike other forms of folk art, the life span of a legend is limited. The age of a false tsar had more or less to match an ordinary mortal's, which is why his legend cannot live much longer than the span of a single generation.

Another question is how faith in the false tsar as redeemer was linked to the actual emergence of real-life false tsars. The general rule was that the birth of the legend had to precede the false tsar's arrival. The false tsar's activities could be relatively successful only if a considerably-strengthened legend assisted him. Usually rumors concerning the emergence of a redeemer were followed by the actual appearance of a false tsar; false tsar's presence was, of course, not an indicator of popular resistance.

Defining the relationship between false tsars and popular movements harbors the possibility of oversimplification. There are a number of cases where false tsars could trigger no mass movements. (Indeed this is true for the overwhelming majority of the cases.) In very general terms, it can be said that all the other conditions had to be present for a pretender and a popular movement to come together. In these cases, however, the false-tsar belief had a revolutionary effect and was able to push the movement further. It provided an aim and an ideology for the social conflict and was sufficient to create an enormous mass base. It is no accident that the greatest uprisings in Russia exploited the opportunities provided by the false-tsar belief. An example in point is Bulavin's revolt. (It must be noted, though, that this remained less significant than the other three great rebellions.) These insurrections, by the way, show a specific development of the false-tsar belief: Bolotnikov waged a regular peasant war in the name of a false tsar who was to appear later; Stepan Razin employed the false-tsar belief only in a supportive capacity. Pugachev, in seeming contrast to the previous line of development, declared himself to be the tsar. Yet this development is still unbroken, expressing the increasing independence—even of the false-tsar belief—of peasant movements. Pugachev was not to serve a false tsar, was not even to look for a medium—he just appointed himself.

Describing the false-tsar phenomenon's geography and social ingredients gives rise to difficult questions. It is probably impossible for us to link the false tsars to definite areas since they emerged in too many locations: however, most often they appeared in the south and southwest. Later, they were increasingly to appear on the peripheries, which are connected to the centralization of the instruments of oppression and control in tribal territories and with the advantages great distances bestowed on the false tsars. As to the impostors' origins, every layer of society was represented, from slave to declassé nobles. In spite of this, it is clear that false tsarhood was an institution typical of the oppressed classes, promoted by upper social layers only in the period when it was being established. All the same, the link between false tsarhood and the Cossacks was to have an outstanding, though not exclusive, role in the institution's establishment and maintenance in Russia.

Finally, possible causes of this, owing to its huge size—specifically Russian historical phenomenon—should be reviewed so as to understand why those peasants' revolts, considered still to be medieval, were launched under the banner of the false-tsar ideology. Research here can hardly boast of definitive findings. Nevertheless, it is fascinating to see that, while different religious cults and sects featured as the ideologies of peasant revolts in the West, Russian clerics were unable to play that role. Though the first important heretic movement, that of the Old Believers which unfolded in a relatively late period, was generally linked with contemporary popular resistance, it failed to provide it with an ideology. The cause may probably be found in the special relations between the state and the Orthodox Church. These ensured privileged position for sovereign who, for all practical purposes, was the actual head of both hierarchies and a man of divine origins for true believers. Since tsardom harbored a strong religious imagery that distinguished between "true" and "false" tsars, action taken against a sovereign also had to take a similar shape. The explanation of why popular resistance fighters appeared in the names of tsars is a rather simple one. In the history of Russia, tsars had a disproportionally large role to play—even, according to the teaching of religion, far greater than their Western counterparts usually had. A tsar's only real competitor was, therefore, another tsar more"genuine" than he.

So far this has been hardly a complete explanation, since it has concentrated on only one side of the false-tsar phenomenon. It would be an error to view this peculiar social institution only from the political angle even though we cannot deny that the false-tsar faith was a militant ideal, for a long time acting as the ideology of resistance in Russia. Yet that is only part of the truth. The false-tsar phenomenon is much more complex and is not necessarily related to politics. Even in the very beginning there emerged simple impostors whose number grew with the passing of time; we do not have to elevate their activities to the over-worked concept of class conflict.

In reality, the false-tsar practice split right after its birth. One of its two forms used cheating as a weapon in politics; the other used it for its own sake. We cannot even say that exploiting the tsar's name presupposes trickery. From as far back as the seventeenth century, we know of the "tsar game" in contemporary folklore material. Though the authorities cruelly punished those who played it, it was an innocent carnival pastime in which the participants elected a "tsar" from among themselves. Some people may, perhaps, have taken the game too seriously and tried to play on after the festivities. Others learned the art of making false tsars out of Cossacks; others still took the idea and strength from the legend of the redeemer.

Today it would be hopeless to try and reconstruct the psychology of the receiving medium, which is somewhat easier to describe though. The relationship between the typical popular mood and self-appointed rulers in times of intensified social conflicts is a well-explored field, and much has been said about it. But rarely do we find mention of the common mass psychological basis of the two ("political" and "criminal") kinds of false tsardom. Perhaps this is because of its banality. It is nothing other than sinful human naivity, snobbery and irrational respect for authority. Those characteristics can be found among the hundreds of thousands following Pugachev just as much as among those who fell for the genius Ostap Bender left to us by Ilf and Petrov.

Of course, it would be a mistake to link, say, Razin and the Hlestakovs or Benders on the basis of the similarity in patterns of cheating. This account is devoted to the first type, consisting of those people who found the only possible form of resistance— even if dressed in a clown's costume—under specific Russian conditions. The obscurantist tricks of their weak, modern imitators, content even with names like that of Lieutenant Schmidt, are none the less interesting; but they are more the stuff of tabloid newspapers. Pugachev and those like him wrote history for themselves: a chapter of the social conflict between the "haves" and "have nots" in Russia.

? all according powers

NOTES

CHAPTER 1:   THE TERRIBLE "GOOD TSAR"

1. Samuel Collins, *The Present State of Russia, In a letter to a Friend at London* (London, 1671), pp. 51–52.

2. See M. Perrie, "The Popular Image of Ivan the Terrible," *The Slavonic and East European Review* 56, no. 2 (1978).

3. On the historiography of Ivan IV, see Gyula Szvák, "Ot Karamzina do Solov'ieva. K voprosu evoliutsii obraza Ivana IV v russkoi istoriografii," *Annales* (Budapest) 21 (1981): 219–236; Gyula Szvák, "Obraz Ivana IV v russkoi istoriografii vtoroi poloviny XIX–nachala XX vv.'," *Annales* (Budapest) 22 (1982):135–150; Gyula Szvák, "Sovietskaia istoriografiia reform serediny XVI v.'," *Annales* (Budapest) 24 (1985):217–236; Gyula Szvák, "Vopros istoricheskogo znacheniia oprichniny v sovietskoi istoricheskoi nauke," *Studia Slavica*, nos. 1–4 (1987):327–360.

4. See Leonid Iuzefovich, *Samye znamenitye samozvantsy* (Moscow, 1999), pp. 57–74.

5. Ibid., pp. 43–54.

6. See János Barta, *A kétfejű sas árnyékában: az abszolutizmustól a felvilágosodásig, 1711–1780* (Budapest, 1984), pp. 108–109.

CHAPTER 2:   A FRAUD ON THE THRONE

1. Konrad Bussov, *Moskovskaia khronika 1584–1613* (Moscow-Leningrad, 1961), p. 94.

2. R. G. Skrynnikov, *Rossiia v nachale XVII veka. "Smuta"* (Moscow, 1988), p. 100.

3. See the analysis of the several versions A. A. Zimin, *V kanun groznych potriasenii. Predposylki pervoi krestianskoi voiny v Rossii* (Moscow, 1986), pp. 153–182.

4. Bussov, *Moskovskaia khronika*, p. 94.

5. Skrynnikov, *Rossiia*, p. 121.

6. Paul Pierling, *Dmitrii Samozvanets* (Moscow, 1910), pp. 73–74.

7. Stalislaw Zólkiewski, *Expedition to Moscow, a Memoir* (London, 1959), p. 39; Skrynnikov, *Rossiia*, pp. 122–123, 125–126.

8. Pierling, *Dmitrii Samozvanets*, p. 96.

9. Ibid., pp. 95–96.

10. Ibid., p. 64.

11. Lev Vladimirovich Cherepnin, ed., *Skazaniie Avraamiia Palitsyna* (Moscow-Leningrad, 1955), p. 111.

12. *Sbornik Russkogo istoricheskogo obshchestva*, t. 137, pp. 176–177, 247.

13. Skrynnikov, *Rossiia*, pp. 83–100.

14. See E. C. Brody, *The Demetrius Legend and Its Literary Treatment in the Age of Baroque* (Rutherford, N.J.: 1972), pp. 36–51; Philip L. Barbour, *Dimitry Called the Pretender Tsar and Great Prince of All Russia, 1605–1606* (Boston, 1966), pp. 317–319.

15. See Vladimir Borisovich Kobrin, *Ivan Groznyi* (Moscow, 1989), pp. 120–126; R. G. Skrynnikov, *Tsarstvo terrora* (St. Petersburg, 1992), pp. 508–518.

16. See R. G. Skrynnikov, *Boris Godunov* (Moscow, 1979).

17. R. G. Skrynnikov, *Samozvantsy v Rossii v nachale XVII veka. Grigorii Otrepiev* (Moscow, 1987), pp. 51–52.
18. Gyula Szvák, *Cárok és kalandorok. A zavaros időszak története* (Budapest, 1982), pp. 99–100.
19. Skrynnikov, *Samozvantsy*, p. 99.
20. Russia. Arkheograficheskaia komissiia, *Skazaniia inostrannykh pisatelei o Rossii* (St. Petersburg, 1868), 2: 137.
21. Skrynnikov, *Rossiia*, pp. 243–244.
22. R. G. Skrynnikov, *Istoriia Rossiiskaia IX–XVII vekov* (Moscow, 1997), pp. 406–407.
23. Bussov, *Moskovskaia khronika*, p. 120.

CHAPTER 3:   FAKE FALSE TSARS

1. B. A. Uspenskii, "Tsar i samozvanets: samozvanchestvo v Rossii kak kulturno-istoricheskii fenomen," *Izbrannye trudy* (Moscow, 1994), p. 92.
2. Russia. Arkheograficheskaia komissiia, *Skazaniia*, 2:211.
3. Margeret, Jacques, *The Russian Empire and Grand Duchy of Muscovy: A 17th Century French Account* (Pittsburgh, 1983), pp. 74.
4. Bussov, *Moskovskaia khronika*, pp. 138–139.
5. Sergei Fedorovich Platonov, *Ocherki po istorii smuty v Moskovskom gosudarstve XVI–XVII vekov* (Moscow, 1937), pp. 252–257.
6. I. I. Smirnov, *Vosstaniie Bolotnikova. 1606–1607* (Moscow, 1951), pp. 365–373.
7. Platonov, *Ocherki po istorii smuty*, pp. 259–260.
8. Bussov, *Moskovskaia khronika*, pp. 144–145.
9. S. M. Troitskii, "Samozvantsy v Rossii XVII–

XVIII vv.," *Voprosy Istorii*, no. 3 (1969): 137–138; R. G. Skrynnikov, *Minin i Pozharskii* (Moscow, 1981), p. 104.

10. Russia. Arkheograficheskaia komissiia, *Skazaniia*, 2:248.

11. Lev Vladimirovich Cherepnin, ed., *Skazanie Avraamiia Palitsyna* (Moscow, 1955), pp. 117–119.

12. Aleksander Hirschberg, *Maryna Mniszchówna* (Moscow, 1908), pp. 92–100.

13. Skrynnikov, *Minin i Pozharskii*, pp. 111–112.

14. Zólkiewski, *Expedition to Moscow*, pp. 60–65.

15. Ibid., pp. 93–98.

16. Ibid., p. 117.

17. Skrynnikov, *Minin i Pozharskii*, pp. 220–225.

18. Ibid., pp. 283–295.

19. See Aleksander Lazarevich Stanislavskii, *Grazhdanskaia voina v Rossii XVII v.: kazachestvo na perelome istorii* (Moscow, 1990), pp. 46–79.

CHAPTER 4:   IMPOSTORS ABROAD

1. See Gyula Szvák, *A Moszkvai Oroszország története* (Budapest, 1997), pp. 81–89.

2. Sergei Mikhailovich Soloviev, *Istoriia Rossii s drevneishich vremen* (Moscow, 1960) 5:569–570.

3. Ibid., p. 249.

4. Ibid., p. 251.

5. Kirill Vasil'evich Chistov, *Russkie narodnye sotsial'no–utopicheskie legendy XVII–XIX vv.* (Moscow, 1967), p. 66.

6. Sergei Mikhailovich Soloviev, *Sochineniia*, (Moscow, 1990), 5:445–446.

7. Ibid., 5:446.

8. Iuzefovich, *Samye znamenitye samozvantsy*, pp. 176–178.

9. V. A. Moshin, "Iz istorii snoshenii rimskoi kurii, Rossii i iuzhnych slavian," *Mezhdunarodnyie sviazi Rossii do XVII v.* (Moscow, 1961), pp. 491–511.

10. Soloviev, *Sochineniia*, 5:235–240.

11. Ibid., 5:542–544.

12. Ibid., 5:546–548.

13. Ibid., 5:583–586.

14. Ibid., 5:585–586.

15. Ibid., 5:587.

16. Ibid., 5:585.

17. Chistov, *Russkiie narodnyie*, pp. 77–78.

CHAPTER 5:   THE COSSACK LEADER AND THE INVISIBLE
FALSE TSAREVICH

1. See Szvák, *A Moszkvai Oroszország története*, pp. 81–101.

2. Ibid., p. 123.

3. Nikolai Fedorovich Kapterev, *Patriarkh Nikon i tsar Aleksei Michailovich, Tri veka. Rossiia ot smuty do nashego vremeni* (Moscow, 1912), 2:255–274;   Anton Vladimirovich Kartashev, *Ocherki po istorii russkoi tserkvi* (Moscow, 1992), 2: 209–218;   Philip Longworth, *Alexis. Tsar of All the Russias* (London, 1984), pp. 104, 112, 122–131.

4. Aleksandr Evgenevich Presniakov, *Rossiiskiie samoderzhtsy* (Moscow, 1990), pp. 90–91.

5. V. N. Storozhev, *Boiarstvo i dvorianstvo v XVII, Tri veka,* 2:219–225.

6. V. Ia. Ulanov, *Razinovshchina, Tri veka* (Moscow, 1912), 1:238–241.

7. Ibid., 1:243.

8. Andrei Nikolaevich Sakharov, *Stepan Razin (Khronika XVII v.)* (Moscow, 1973), pp. 31–48.

9. Ibid., pp. 60–61.

10. Arkadii Georgievich Man'kov, ed., *Inostrannye izvestiia o vosstanii Stepana Razina: materialy i issledovaniia* (Leningrad, 1975), pp. 166–174.

11. Andrei Nikolaevich Sakharov, ed., *Istoriia Rossii. S drevneishich vremien do kontsa XVII veka* (Moscow, 1996), p. 538.

12. Sakharov, *Stepan Razin*, pp. 172–174.

13. E. A. Shvetsova, ed., *Krestianskaia voina pod predvoditelstvom Stepana Razina: sbornik dokumentov* (Moscow, 1954), 1:235.

14. Soloviev, *Istoriia Rossii*, p. 539.

15. Chistov, *Russkiie narodnyie*, pp. 80–82.

16. Viktor Ivanovich Buganov, *Krest'ianskie voiny v Rossii semnadtsatogo–vosemnadsatogo vv.* (Moscow, 1976), p. 111. Other sources also stress Razin's heroism, yet his last words addressed to his brother were "Shot up you dog!" See Man'kov, *Inostrannye izvestiia*, pp. 74–75, 79.

17. Arkadii Georgievich Man'kov, ed., *Zapiski inostrantsev o vosstanii Stepana Razina* (Leningrad, 1968), p. 113.

18. Soloviev, *Istoriia Rossii*, 3:133–134.

19. Nikolai Ivanovich Kostomarov, *Samozvantsy i proroki: isstoricheskie monografii i issleddovaniia* (Moscow, 1997), p. 193.

20. Ibid., pp. 194–197.

CHAPTER 6:   THE ANTICHRIST TSAR AND HIS FALSE
              SONS

1. See Sergei Fedorovich Platonov, *Moskva i Zapad* (Berlin, 1926), pp. 115–126, 140–146.

2. R. K. Massie, *Peter the Great. His Life and World* (London, 1982), pp. 155–202.

3. Nikolai Ivanovich Pavlenko, *Petr Velikii* (Moscow, 1994), pp. 238–249.

4. P. P. Basnin, "Raskolnich'i legendy o Petre Velikom," *Istoricheskii vestnik,* no. 5 (1903):517–520.

5. Grigorii Vasilevich Esipov, *Raskol'nich'i dela XVIII veka* (St. Petersburg, 1861), 2:41.

6. Nina Borisovna Golikova, *Politicheskie protsessy pri Petre pervom* (Moscow, 1957), p. 179.

7. Vasilii Osipovich Kliuchevskii, *Sochineniia* (Moscow, 1958), 4:229.

8. Ibid., 4:39–41.

9. Massie, *Peter the Great*, p. 670.

10. Evgenii Viktorovich Anisimov, *Vremia Petrovskikh reform: XVIII vek. 1-aia chetvert'* (Leningrad, 1989), pp. 442–445.

11. Ibid., pp. 447–457.

12. Golikova, *Politicheskie protsessy*, pp. 176–177.

13. Soloviev, *Istoriia Rossii*, 9:190.

14. Chistov, *Russkie narodnye*, p. 124.

15. Ibid., pp. 124–125.

CHAPTER 7:   EMPRESSES, MINIONS, IMPOSTORS

1. Pavlenko, *Petr Velikii*, pp. 554–560.

2. Nikolai Ivanovich Pavlenko, *Aleksandr Danilovich Menshikov* (Moscow, 1981), p. 30.

3. See Evgenii Viktorovich Anisimov, *Rossiia bez Petra. 1725–1740* (St. Petersburg, 1994), pp. 144–151, 169–171.

4. See Evgenii Viktorovich Anisimov, *Zhenshchiny na Rossiiskom prestole* (St. Petersburg, 1997), pp. 69–274.

5. Katherine's rise to the throne was made possible by Peter III's death. It is unlikely, however, that she gave

direct orders to have him murdered. See Aleksandr B. Kamenskii, *Zhizn'i sud'ba imperatritsy Ekateriny Velikoi* (Moscow, 1997), pp. 68–82.

6. Chistov, *Russkie narodnye*, p. 126.

7. Ibid., pp. 127–128.

8. Soloviev, *Istoriia Rossii*, 10:661–662.

9. Chistov, *Russkie narodnye*, pp. 129–130.

10. Ibid., p. 132.

11. Kamenskii, *Zhizn'i sud'ba*, p. 97.

12. K. V. Sivkov, "Samozvanchestvo v Rossii v poslednei treti XVIII v.," *Istoricheskiie zapiski*, 31 (1950):100–102.

13. See V. Naumov, "Petr III," in *Romanovy: istoricheskiie portrety*, ed. Andrei Nikolaevich Sakharov (Moscow, 1997), pp. 558–600.

14. Sivkov, "Samozvanchestvo v Rossii," p. 96.

15. Chistov, *Russkie narodnye*, p. 140.

16. Sivkov, "Samozvanchestvo v Rossii," pp. 97–98.

17. Ibid, pp. 103–108.

18. Ibid, pp. 108–111.

19. Ibid, p. 112.

CHAPTER 8:   A FOLK HERO IN THE ROBE OF A TSAR

1. See Mikhail Mikhailovich Shcherbatov, *O povrezhdenii nravov v Rossii /kniazia Shcherbatova i Puteshestvie/ Radishcheva* (Moscow, 1984).

2. See Emil Niederhauser, "Catherine II and Enlightened Absolutism," in *Mesto Rossii v Evrope*, ed. Gyula Szvák (Budapest, 1999), pp. 236–239.

3. *Entsiklopediia Brokgauza i Efrona* (Moscow, 1992), 26:209.

4. Sivkov, "Samozvanchestvo v Rossii," pp. 117–120.

5. Ibid, pp. 113–117.

6. Buganov, *Krest'ianskie voiny v Rossii*, pp. 171–175.

7. See Viktor Ivanovich Buganov, *Pugachev* (Moscow, 1984), pp. 5–28.

8. A. I. Andrushchenko, "O samozvantstve E. I. Pugacheva i ego otnosheniiah s iaitskimi kazakami," in *Voprosy sotsialno–ekonomicheskoi istorii i istochnikovedeniia perioda feodalizma v Rossii* (Moscow, 1961), pp. 146–150.

9. Viktor Ivanovich Buganov, ed., *Krest'ianskaia voina v Rossii v 1773–1775 godah. Vosstaniie Pugacheva* (Moscow, 1966), 2:94; H. I. Muratov, *Krest'ianskaia voina v 1773–1775 gg. v Rossii* (Moscow, 1954), p. 32.

10. Ibid., pp. 102–103.

11. Buganov, *Krest'ianskie voiny v Rossii*, pp. 182–189.

12. Ibid., pp. 181, 183, 187.

13. Chistov, *Russkie narodnye*, p. 167.

14. Ibid., p. 173.

15. Buganov, *Krest'ianskie voiny v Rossii*, pp. 202–207.

16. Ibid., pp. 215–217.

17. Sergei Aleksandrovich Golubtsov, ed. *Pugachevshchina. Sbornik dokumentov* (Moscow–Leningrad, 1929), 2:197–198.

18. Chistov, *Russkie narodnye*, p. 172.

19. Buganov, *Pugachev*, pp. 362–365.

20. Sivkov, "Samozvanchestvo v Rossii," pp. 120–122.

21. See S. S. Lur'e, "Kniazhna Tarakanova," *Voprosy istorii*, no. 10 (1966):207–210.

22. Chistov, *Russkie narodnye*, pp. 175–177.

23. Ibid., p. 177.

24. Sivkov, "Samozvanchestvo v Rossii," p. 133.

25. Ibid., pp. 123–125.

26. See Daniil Lukich Mordovtsev, *Sobranie sochinenii* (St. Petersburg, 1901), 17:142–151.

27. Chistov, *Russkie narodnye*, pp. 181–183.

28. See Aleksandr Sergeevich Myl'nikov, *Legenda o russkom printse: russko-slavienskie sviazi XVIII v. v mire narodnoi kul'tury* (Leningrad, 1987), pp. 34–61.

CHAPTER 9:   THE LEGEND DIES

1. See N. V. Riasanovsky, *A History of Russia*, 5th ed. (New York, Oxford, 1993), pp. 274–275; Natan Iakovlevich Eidelman, *Gran'vekov: politicheskaia bor'ba v Rossii: konets XVIII-nachalo XIX stoleetiia* (Moscow, 1982).

2. Eidelman, *Gran' vekov*, pp. 305–326.

3. Chistov, *Russkie narodnye*, p. 185.

4. See Andrei Nikolaevich Sakharov, *Aleksandr I* (Moscow, 1998), pp. 115–166.

5. Chistov, *Russkie narodnye*, p. 197.

6. Sakharov, *Aleksandr I*, pp. 10–12.

7. Ibid., pp. 12–14;

8. Riasanovsky, *A History of Russia*, pp. 300–302.

9. See L. Liubimov, "Taina startsa Fedora Kuzmicha," *Voprosi istorii*, no. 1 (1966); S. B. Okun', N. N. Belianchikov, "Sushchestvuiet li 'taina Fedora Kuzmicha'?," *Voprosi istorii*, no. 1 (1967):191–201.

10. Andrei Nikolaevich Sakharov, ed., *Istoriia Rossii s nachala XVIII do kontsa XIX* (Moscow, 1996), pp. 331–332.

11. Chistov, *Russkie narodnye*, pp. 198–204.

12. Daniil Lukich Mordovtsev, "Odin iz Lzhekonstantinov," in *Sobraniie sochinenii* (St. Petersburg, 1901), 19: 6–7.

13. B. Kubalov, "Sibir' i samozvantsy. Iz istorii narodnych volnenii v XIX v.," *Sibirskiie ogni*, no. 3 (1924):174–176.

14. Chistov, *Russkie narodnye*, p. 206.

15. Ibid., pp. 208–209.

16. Ibid., pp. 209–211.

17. See Riasanovsky, *A History of Russia*, pp. 369–374.

18. Chistov, *Russkie narodnye*, p. 214.

19. Ibid., pp. 214–216.

20. Vladimir Galaktionovich Korolenko, "Sovremennaia samozvanshchina," in *Polnoe sobraniie sochinenii* (St. Petersburg, 1914), 3: 337–338.

21. Ibid., pp. 340–341.

22. Ibid., pp. 341–342.

CHAPTER 10:   FROM TSAR GRISHKA TO OSTAP BENDER

1. Major sources for this summary chapter were the volumes of Kirill Vasil'evich Chistov, Natan Iakovlevich Eidelman, and Boris Andreevich Uspenski—all cited in the previous chapters. I also have found most useful the following two monographs: Aleksandr Mikhailovich Panchenko, *Russkaia kul'tura v kanun Petrovskikh reform* (Leningrad, 1984) and Paul Avrich, *Russian Rebels, 1600–1800* (New York, 1972).

EUROPEAN RUSSIA 1533–1598

INDEX

A

Afanasy Petrovich, 132
Akundinov, Timoshka (Timofey, Timotei), 53–58
Alexander I, tsar, 131–137
Alexander II, tsar, 141
Alexander the Great, 22
Alexeyev, Petr (Petr Mikhailov, Peter I), 89
Alexis, false tsarevich, 76–77, 87, 98, 101
Alexis, tsar, 54, 62–64, 70
Alexis, tsarevich, 72, 74, 76–77, 87
Alexis Petrovich, 90–94, 96
Andreyev, soldier, 127
Anne Ivanovna, tsarina, 96–98
Anne Petrovna, daughter of Peter I, 97
Antonovitch, Ivan, tsar, 102, 126
Artiemniev, Yevstify, 94
Arzamas, 76
Aslanbekov, Anton, 105
Astrabad, 69
Astrakhan, 32, 41, 45, 52, 56, 67, 70, 72–73, 75
Austria, 54
Azov Sea, 65–66, 71, 82, 89

B

Bacchus, 90
Baku, 69
Bashkiria, 117, 119–120

Batiushkov, ensign, 111
Belinsky, Polish nobleman, 49
Bender, Ostap, 146–147, 152
Bering expedition, 101
Bezdna, 141–142
Biron, Ernst Johann, duke, 96
Black Sea, 65
Bodirin, Fedor, ataman, 32
Bogomolov, Fedot (Kazin), 112, 115–116
Bolotnikov, Ivan, 29–37, 150
Brandenburg, 56
Brest-Litovsk, 48–49
Bucinski, Jan, 23
Bulavin, Kondrati, hetman, 83, 149–150
Bulgaria, 53
Bussow, Konrad, 9, 30, 35–36
Butirin, peasant, 145

C   Caspian Sea, 32, 66
Catherine I, tsarina, 98
Catherine II (the Great), tsarina, 97, 102, 110–
        111, 114, 122, 124–125, 131–132
Chelyabinsk, 139
Cherkassk, 67, 71,
Cherkassky, Andrei, prince, 74
Chernigov, 105
Chernishev, Petr, 106, 119
Chigirin, 144
Chudov, monastery, 14
Claude, (false Jeanne d'Arc), 5
Clement VIII, pope, 12
Collins, Samuel, 3
Constantine Pavlovich, grand duke, 137–141,
        144, 147

Constantinople, 51–53, 56, 88
Cossacks, 15–20, 29–30, 32–34, 37–38, 40–45, 47,
     50–52, 54–55, 61, 64–79, 83, 101, 112–
     119, 123–125, 128, 140, 143
     Don, 78, 100–101, 112, 114, 116, 121–124,
         127–128,
     Kazan, 115
     Terek, 115
     Ukrainian, 78
     Ural, 129
     Volga, 127
     Yaik, 113–115, 121, 123
     Zaporozhe, 78
Courland, 96
Cracow, 10, 12–13
Crimea, 50–51
Croesus, king, 12

D   Decembrists, 138
     Derbent, 69
     Dirikov, Ivan, 101
     Dmitri, real and false tsarevich, 8–15, 17–24, 27–
         38, 40–41, 43–45, 48– 50, 53, 58
     Dmitrievich, Ivan, 48
     Dnieper, river, 78
     Dobrinitch, 19
     Dolgoruky, Yuri, prince, 67, 75
     Don, river, 33, 50, 65–67, 70–71, 73, 75, 78, 112–
         114, 116, 119–124, 126–128
     Donets, river, 50, 73
     Doroshenko, Petr, hetman, 78
     Dosifeya, nun, 125
     Dubovka, 112, 127

E   Egypt, 4, 116
           Elizabeth Petrovna, tsarina, 97, 101–102, 111,
                  124–125
           Europe, 4, 58, 115, 141

F   Farahabad, 69
           Fedor Borisovich, tsarevich, 20
           Fedor Ivanovich, tsar, 8, 16, 53
           Fedor Fedorovich, false tsarevich, 38
           Filaret, Patriarch, 39, 62–63
           France, 138
           Frederick the Great, king, 104
           Friedrich, prince, 56

G   Galich, 13
           Gatchina, 131
           Gavrila, false tsarevich, 41
           Godunov, Boris, tsar, 8–13, 16, 18–21, 81
           Gogol, Nikolai Vasilevich, 144
           Gorokhovaya, village, 140
           Goshcha, 7, 11
           Govoruha, Matriona, 67

H   Hanin, Maxim, 127–128
           Henry VII, king, 5
           Herodotus, 12
           Hlestakovs, 152
           Hoisky, nobleman, 7
           Holstein, 56, 127
           Holy Land, 14
           Holy See, 25

Hromov, estate, 135
Hronov, merchant, 135
Hungary, 5, 54–55

I   Ilf, 150
Ingermansland, 104
Ivan IV (the Terrible), tsar, 1, 3–4, 36, 41, 44,
         148
Ivan V, co-tsar, 82, 96
Ivan VI (Antonovich), tsar, 97, 102, 104
Ivan (Jan Luba), 49–50,
Ivan-August, false tsarevich, 41
Ivangorod, 43
Ivanovich, Vasily, 55

J   Jerusalem, 88, 116
Joakhim, archimandrita, 50

K   Kaffa, 50
Kagalnitsky, village, 70
Kalmyks, 16, 67
Kaluga, 32–34, 42, 44, 50
Kalugin, false tsarevich, 140
Kama, river, 119
Kamchatka, 101, 136
Karazeisky, Ivan, 56
Karpogol, 102
Kazan, 112, 115, 120–121, 123
Khlopko, 17
Khmelnitsky, Bogdan, 55
Kiev, 7, 9, 101, 104, 116, 123, 138

Kirghiz, 140
Kirillovna, Natalya, 88
Kiselev, Paul, count, 139
Klementy, false tsarevich, 41
Kleopin, Ivan, 77
Klyuchevsky, Vasily, 90
Klyukin, Ivan, 140
Kola peninsula, 127
Kolomenskoye, 64
Kolomna, 13
Komaritskaya, district, 36
Koniyuhovsky, Kostka, 56–57
Korea, 138
Korneyev, veteran, 138
Krasnoufimsk, district, 134, 136
Krasnoyarsk, 132
Krekshin, Andrei, 93
Kremlin, 20, 24, 31, 42–44, 89, 98
Kremniov, Gavrila, 105–106
Kretov, Nikolay, captain, 111, 137
Kromi, 19–20
Kuban, area, 115
Kurbsky, Andrei, prince, 36
Kursk, 105, 127
Kuzmich, Fyodor, 134-137

L   Lavrenty, false tsarevich, 41
Lefort, François, 85, 88–89
Liapunov, Prokopi, 31–32
Lithuania, 9–10, 13–15, 18, 30, 40, 47, 56–57
Livonia, 15
Lopotsky, gentleman, 1
Luba, Dmitri, 49–50, 53
Luba, Jan (Ivan), 49–50,

Lubeck, 55

M   Malta, 127
           Maly, Stepan, 129
           Marienburg, 95
           Martin, false tsarevich, 41
           Matveyev, Ivan, 102
           Maurin, false prince, 146
           Menshikov, Prince Alexander, 92, 94, 96
           Metelkin, (Sweeper), folk hero, 126
           Mezshevaya Utka, 87
           Mian Kaleh, 69
           Michael Fiodorovich, tsar, 45, 50, 5, 62
           Miechowicki, Polish nobleman, 35, 37
           Mikhailov, Ivan (Yevdokimov), 103
           Mikhailov, Petr (Peter I), 89
           Mikhelson, Ivan, 120
           Miloslavsky, boyar, 77
           Minin, Kuzma, 44, 61
           Minitsky, false tsarevich, 101
           Mirovich, Vasily, 102
           Mitka, Cossack, 32–33
           Miyussky, hetman, 78
           Mniszech, Jerzy, 10–12, 23, 30, 35–36, 39–40
           Mniszech, Marina, 11
           Moghilev, 35
           Molchanov, Mikhail, 28, 30, 34–35
           Moldavia, 48, 52, 54
           Montenegro, 129
           Moscow, 13–15, 17, 19–21, 23–24, 28–34, 38–44,
                 48, 53–56, 62–63, 65–68, 71–74, 76–79,
                 87–89, 92, 94, 96, 101, 109, 112, 120, 122–
                 123, 125, 128, 144
           Mosyaghin, peasant, 124

Münnich, Burkhard, count, 96
Muromets, Ileika (Gorchakov), 33

N   Nagaia, Maria, 21, 28
           Nagoy, clan, 35
           Naples, 92
           Napoleon, Emperor of France, 133
           Narodniks, 144
           Narva, 55,127, 138
           Nerchinsk, 106
           Neva, river, 84, 95–96
           Nizhegorod, district, 75, 93, 103,
           Nicholas I, tsar, 134, 137–138, 140
           Nicholas II, tsar, 134
           Nikon, patriarch, 63, 74
           Novgorod, 41, 43–44
                   Nizhny-, 44
                   -Seversky, 18
           Novospassky, convent, 125

O   Olga, duchess, 97
           Opochinin, adjutant, 111
           Orenburg, 111, 114, 117, 119–120, 140
           Orlov, Alexis, 110, 124
           Oruzheynikov, Cossack, 128
           Oryol, 36
           Osinovik, false tsarevich, 41
           Ostermann, Andrew, count, 96
           Otrepiev, (-Smirnov), 13
           Otrepiev, Gregory, (Grishka, Yushka), 4, 13, 18–
                   19, 22, 24, 28–29, 37

P

Panin, Petr Ivanovich, count, 124
Panshin, village, 71
Paris, 124
Pashkov, Istoma, 31–32
Patrikeyev, chief clerk, 57
Paul I, tsar, 131
Paul, tsarevich, 122–123, 126
Pavlovna, Maria, 139
Perevolok, 67, 71
Pereyaslavl, 78
Persia, 56, 124
Peshkov, Ivan, 57
Petchersky monastery, 7
Peter, false tsar, 105,
Peter, false tsarevich, 32–33, 36, 38, 41
Peter I, tsar, 81–98, 101, 109, 115, 149
Peter II, tsar, 96, 98, 103, 126
Peter III (also Karl Ulrich) real and false tsar, 97,
          101, 104–107, 111–113, 115–116, 119,
          122–124, 126–129, 131–132, 147
Peter Fyodorovich, 128
Peter Petrovich, false tsarevich, 99, 100–102
Peter-Paul, fortress, 125, 133, 138
Petrov, Anton, 141–142
Petrovich, Afanasy, 132
Pianov, Cossack, 115
Platonida, nun, 87
Pleshtcheyev, boyar, 63
Pochep, town, 94
Poland, 9–10, 15, 18, 30, 36, 39–40, 47–50, 54–
          55, 64–65, 115–116
Potemkin, Gregory, prince, 110
Pozharsky, Dmitri, 44
Prokhorov, peasant, 128

Protopopov, Nikolay, 139
Prozorovsky, Ivan, prince, 54
Prussia, 104
Pskov, 43–44, 56
Pugachev, Emelian, 107, 111, 114–124, 126– 129,
    148, 150, 152
Putivl, 19–20, 31–33, 54

R   Radishchev, Alexander, 109, 111
        Rákóczi, Ferenc II, prince, 5,
        Rákóczi, George, prince, 55–56
        Rangoni, Claudio, papal nuncio, 12
        Razin, Stepan (Stenka), 59, 66–68, 70–79, 150, 152
        Razumovsky, Alexis, 124–125
        Razumovsky, Kiril, 125
        Red Square, 27, 76
        Revel, 55
        Rodionov, Alexis, 94
        Romanov dynasty, 13, 39, 44–45, 62, 140
        Rome, 4, 53–54, 56, 88
        Russia, 4–5, 27, 30, 36–37, 39–40, 42, 47–49, 52,
            58, 61–64, 71, 81–83, 85–86, 93–94, 97,
            103–104, 110, 113–115, 124, 129, 137–138,
            143, 147–148, 150–152

S   Samara, 33, 75, 128, 144–145
        Sambor, castle, 10–12, 30
        Samoylovich, hetman, 77–78
        Sapieha, Jan Petr, 38
        Saratov, 75, 138, 141, 144–146
        Savelov, Gerasim, 127
        Savely, false tsarevich, 41
        Schlüsserburg, 102

Schmidt, Lieutenant, 152

Sciuiski, Gion, 53

Sebastian, king, 12

Sein, general, 89

Selivanov, Kondrati, 129

Semikov, Aleksandr, 94

Semyon, false tsarevich, 41, 56

Semyonovsky, monastery, 49

Serbia, 53

Serko, hetman, 77–78

Seversk, 40

Shakhovskoi, prince, 28, 30–31, 33–34

Shirinsky-Shikhmatov, false prince, 146

Shuisky, Dmitri, 36, 38

Shuisky, Semion, 53

Shuisky, Vasily, tsar, 21, 27–29, 31, 33–34, 36,
            39, 41–42, 51–58

Shuisky, Yoan Timofey Vladimir, 53

Siberia, 100–101, 109, 112, 114, 119, 124, 129,
            132, 134, 136, 139–140

Sidorka, (Matyushka), 43–44

Sigismund III, king, 9, 12, 36, 39, 42, 48–49

Simbirsk, 75

Simeon, tsarevich, 72, 77–79

Simnel, Lambert, 5

Skavronska, Katerina, 95

Skopin-Shuisky, Prince Mikhael, 41–42

Smolensk, 31, 42–43

Solovetsky, monastery, 67

Sophia, Alekseyevna, 82, 134

St. Andrew, 123

St. Petersburg, 94, 98, 101, 103–104, 109, 111,
            113, 119–120, 122, 124–125, 128, 133,
            135, 146

Starodub, 34–36
Starodubtsev, Larion, 99–100
Stekol (Stockholm), 89
Stekoli, county (Sweden), 89
Streshniev, boyar, 85
Sweden, 41, 55–56
Szegedinac, Pero, 5

T   Taganrog, 134–135, 137
Tambov, 98, 124, 139
Tarakanova, princess, 125
Tartars, 29, 116
Teliatevsky, Andrei, prince, 33
Terek, river, 32–33, 116
Timofey, 53, 58, 66–67, 99
Tobolsk, 87, 101
Tolmachev, brothers, cossacks, 117
Tomsk, 134–136, 145–146
Toropets, 77
Trakhaniotov, boyar, 63
Transylvania, 55
Traubenberg, general, 114
Truzhenik, Timofey, 99–100
Tsaritsyn, 68, 70, 72–73, 112, 115–116, 121
Tsarskoye Selo, 131
Tula, 33–36, 44
Tula, river, 36
Turkey, 115, 138
Turkoman, 69
Tushino, 38–44

U   Uglich, 8, 10, 13–14, 21, 29

Ukraine, 54–55, 62, 77–79, 101, 105
Ulozhenie, 63
Ulrich-Peter, Karl, 101, 106
Unkovsky, Andrei, Voevoda, 55, 68
Urals, 107, 113, 119-120, 128
Urusov, Petr, 43
Us, Vasily, 66
Ushakov, Fedor, 101
Utka, Mezshevaya, 87
Uvarov, nobleman, 136

V   Varlaam, monk, 14
Varvarka Street, 14
Vasily, false tsarevich, 36, 41
Vatican, 53
Vedernikovsky, village, 70
Venice, 30, 53
Vergunyonok, Ivashka, 50–51
Veselkov, Dorofey, 87
Viatka, 139
Viazemsky, prince, 107
Vigovsky, hetman, 56
Volga, river, 32–33, 41, 44, 66–69, 71, 73–75, 107,
        112–115, 117, 119, 121, 126, 144–145
Volhynia, 14
Vologda, 56–57, 94
Vorobyov, Semion, 78–79
Voronezh, 66, 105
Warbeck, Perkin, 4–5
Warsaw, 78
Wisniowiecki, Adam, 7, 9–10
Wisniowiecki, Constantin, 7, 9–10
Wladislaw, prince, 47–48

Y

Yaik, river, 117
Yaitsky, fortress, 68, 114, 117
Yakovlev, Kornilo, hetman, 75
Yeletsky, district, 126
Yenisey, province, 139
Yerofey, false tsarevich, 41

Z

Zagorovsky, monastery, 14
Zaporozhe, 77–78
Zarubin-Chika, Cossack commander, 119–120
Zarutsky, Ivan, hetman, 45
Zemetayev, Ignaty, 126
Zólkiewski, Stanislas, hetman, 42
Zotov, Nikita, 90

ABOUT THE AUTHORS

GYULA SZVÁK is director of the Center for Russian Studies of Eötvös Loránd University of Budapest. He is the leading Hungarian specialist of the Muscovite and Imperial periods in Russian history. His publications include several monographs and numerous essays. This volume is his first English-language monograph.

NICHOLAS V. RIASANOVSKY is Sidney Hellman Ehrman Professor of European History at the University of California, Berkeley. He has been associated with several West European and Soviet centers of Slavic studies, including Moscow, Leningrad, Helsinki, Paris, and London. He is a former president of the American Association for the Advancement of Slavic Studies, and was elected to the American Academy of Arts and Sciences in 1987. He is the author of many books and voluminous articles.